Mill H. Nhum Jr.
Madison   17 April 1980

Japanese Literature in Chinese

[VOLUME II]

Poetry and Prose in Chinese by Japanese Writers of the Later Period

Prepared for the Columbia College Program of Translations from the Oriental Classics

✍ *Japanese Literature in Chinese*

in Chinese

[VOLUME II]

✍ Poetry & Prose in Chinese by Japanese Writers of the Later Period

Translated by Burton Watson

Columbia University Press • New York • 1976

The Japan Foundation, through a special grant, has assisted the Press in publishing this volume.

Library of Congress Cataloging in Publication Data (Revised)
Main entry under title:

Japanese literature in Chinese.

"Translations from the Oriental classics."
CONTENTS: v. 1. Poetry & prose in Chinese by Japanese writers of the early period.—v. 2. Poetry & prose in Chinese by Japanese writers of the later period.
   1. Chinese literature—Translations into English.
2. English literature—Translations from Chinese.
3. Chinese literature—Japanese authors. I. Watson, Burton, 1925–
PL2658.E1J3   895.1'08'001   75-15896
ISBN 0-231-03986-7 (v.1)
ISBN 0-231-04146-2 (v.2)

"Coming Home," "Shortly after I married. . . ," "New House," "Written on New Year's Eve," "I accompanied my uncle . . . ," "Grieving for Tatsuzō . . . ," "Reading Books #3 and #6," "Escorting my mother . . . ," "Delighted that Jippo . . . ," and "A Parting Talk . . ." by Rai Sanyo. Copyright © 1975 by The Montemora Foundation Inc. and reprinted by permission of The Montemora Foundation Inc.

Columbia University Press
New York—Guildford, Surrey

To Matsushita Tadashi

Contents

Introduction   1

Bibliographical Note   20

PART 1

Works from the Fourteenth Century
to the Present   23

PART 2

Works by the Monk Ryōkan   85

PART 3

Works by Rai San'yō   119

PART 4

Works by Natsume Sōseki   171

Index of Authors   191

INTRODUCTION

Japan from early times has had two literatures, one composed in the native language and transmitted orally until a writing system based upon Chinese characters was devised in the eighth century to record it, the other composed in the Chinese language itself and patterned directly on Chinese models. The former, couched in the language of the country and of far greater antiquity, vigor, and continuity, has quite naturally attracted the larger share of attention, being the subject of exhaustive study by both Japanese and foreign scholars, and much of it by now translated into other languages.

It is perhaps time, therefore, that some notice be taken of "the other Japanese literature," the works of prose and poetry written in Chinese by Japanese over the centuries. In a preceding volume, *Japanese Literature in Chinese: Poetry and Prose in Chinese by Japanese Writers of the Early Period*, I offered selected translations from this literature dating from the seventh to the twelfth centuries. The present work is an attempt to pursue the examination by presenting translations of outstanding works of the later period, particularly the eighteenth and nineteenth centuries. Because of the enormous volume of poetry in Chinese dating from this period and the frequently high level of interest and merit it exhibits, however, I have concentrated almost entirely on poetry, allotting less space to prose works than in the earlier volume.

In the introduction to that volume I discussed some of the reasons that impelled the Japanese to try their hand at the composition of prose and verse in a foreign language: the need to compose occasional verse in the course of diplomatic and social exchanges with the Chinese, and with the Koreans and other mainland peoples who employed classical Chinese as a lingua franca; the desire to gain recognition for Japan's cultural and national identity in the sphere of Sinitic influence; and the literary challenge presented by a foreign medium and the possibilities it offered for exploring forms and themes not found in the native literature.

As the first two of these reasons immediately suggest, Japanese interest and enthusiasm for composition in Chinese customarily rose and fell in proportion to the degree of contact the country maintained with the mainland. My earlier volume covered the period when the Japanese rulers dispatched envoys to the Chinese courts of the Sui and T'ang dynasties and kept up close relations with the states of the Korean Peninsula and Pohai in Manchuria. But in 894 diplomatic missions to China were suspended, and in the centuries immediately following, intercourse with the continent dwindled. The Japanese continued on occasion to write prose and poetry in Chinese, presumably because by this time they had come to regard the medium as an integral part of their own literary heritage, but skill in the language declined markedly and all real creativity was channeled toward the field of native poetry and prose.

In the succeeding Kamakura period (1192–1333) the situation reversed dramatically, due largely to the influence of Zen Buddhism. Japanese monks, anxious to acquaint themselves with the teachings of the Ch'an or Zen sect, journeyed to China, often spending many years on the continent, and Chinese Zen masters, responding to invitations from the Japanese authorities, took up residence in Japan. The Japanese monks, with every incentive to master the Chinese language and frequent opportunities to study under Chinese teachers at home or abroad, not surprisingly attained a proficiency in it far surpassing that of most of their earlier countrymen. Following Chinese custom, they wrote quantities of *kanshi* or verse in Chinese, much of it indistinguishable in technical mastery and facility of expression from products of the continent. But for all its linguistic skill, their verse seems, to me at least, on the whole disappointingly stereotyped and impersonal in content. It belongs to the tradition of Chinese Buddhist poetry that had begun so promisingly with men like Wang Wei and Han-shan in the T'ang dynasty, but which by late Sung times, when Zen was introduced to Japan, had sunk into lifeless mannerism. The Japanese priests proved unable to infuse the tradition with any new vitality, perhaps because they seldom attempted to adapt it to specifically Japanese scenes and tastes. The landscapes depicted in their poems are conventionalized to the point where they might be anywhere in eastern Asia, and the Buddhist sentiments which the poems embody, though often intriguingly garbed in the bizarre imagery and paradoxical utterance peculiar to Zen literature, rarely rise above the level of doctrinal platitude.

The prose and poetry in Chinese written by the Zen monks of the Kamakura and the succeeding Muromachi period (1393–1573) came to be known as *Gozan bungaku*, the "Literature of the Five Mountains," in reference to the major Zen temples of Kamakura and Kyoto. In spite of its obvious importance in the history of Japanese literature in Chinese, I have not attempted to deal with it comprehensively in my selection, preferring to devote space to later works that appear to me of greater interest and originality. I have, however, included a few poems that are atypical of the literature as a whole but represent attempts to treat actual events of the time or details of everyday life, early adumbrations of what, many centuries later, were to become the dominant trends of the *kanshi*. A forthcoming volume of translations of Gozan poetry by Marian Ury will, I trust, compensate for my neglect in this respect and allow the English reader to sample representative works of the period.

Though the Zen monks during the middle ages, as we have

3

seen, were assiduous writers of verse, and to a less extent prose, in Chinese—and in the process played a crucial role in introducing new philosophical and literary currents from the mainland—they were almost the only group in Japanese society so engaged. The imperial court, which in Nara and early Heian times had taken the lead in fostering Chinese studies, now devoted its attention almost exclusively to the native literature, particularly *waka* poetry, and the military leaders of the Kamakura and Muromachi shogunates lacked the learning or inclination to compose in Chinese, employing Zen monks as their intermediaries when they found it necessary to communicate with the continent. Consequently, though the aristocracy occasionally employed the medium as a kind of literary pastime, there are virtually no *kanshi* of importance written by secular men from the end of the Heian in the twelfth century to the founding of the Tokugawa shogunate in 1603. After that date, however, the situation began to alter radically.

The Tokugawa shoguns, in an effort to lend prestige to their rule and to promote social stability and public morality, adopted the Neo-Confucian school of philosophy as the official doctrine of the state and actively encouraged Confucian studies, founding a college devoted to such studies in Edo, the seat of the shogunate. Similar schools were in time established under official auspices in a number of the important fiefs, while many scholars in the large cities opened private schools to teach Confucianism, though often in ways that deviated from the Chu Hsi interpretation endorsed by the state. Thus a considerable number of Japanese, particularly of the samurai class, came to devote themselves intensively to the study of the Confucian Classics and of Chinese literature in general (though cut off from any direct contact with the continent by the strict seclusion policy of the government), and the proportion of men capable of writing

4

prose and verse in Chinese greatly increased. So began the third great era of *kanshi* writing in Japanese history, not the creation of court officials and aristocrats, as in the Nara and Heian eras, nor of monks, as in the case of Gozan literature, but of scholarly-minded samurai, usually of lower social standing, and occasionally of learned priests of various Buddhist sects.

The most appropriate periodization to be adopted in dealing with the history of Tokugawa *kanshi* is still a matter of debate, as are many other aspects of the subject, since it has yet to receive intensive study either in Japan or abroad.[1] It is generally agreed that *kanshi* writing was not of great importance during the first hundred years of Tokugawa rule, and few works of outstanding merit remain from this period. For one thing, scholars of the time had in many cases not yet acquired sufficient mastery of Chinese to allow them to write verse effectively and with ease. In addition, many of them, seconding the view of Chinese Neo-Confucians themselves, looked upon the writing of poetry as frivolous or outright reprehensible, a deflection of energies from the more vital concerns of philosophy, ethics, and statecraft. Some, such as Kaibara Ekken (1630–1714), who was particularly concerned with translating the verities of Neo-Confucianism into terms that could be understood by Japanese of all levels of society, condemned it as mere foolishness, declaring that "Japanese poetry is quite sufficient for setting forth one's ideas and

1. Matsushita Tadashi, in his invaluable work *Edo jidai no shifū shiron* ("*Kanshi* Theory and Style in the Edo Period") (Tokyo: Meiji shoin, 1969), pp. 6–12, reviews earlier theories of periodization, most of which favor a three-part division. Matsushita suggests a four-part division of his own. My remarks, for reasons that will become apparent, are based on a rough three-part division: (1) 1603–c.1710; (2) c.1710–c.1780; (3) c.1780–1867. Matsushita divides the final period into two, for reasons that are sound but too subtle to be reflected in my selection.

5

expressing one's emotions in this country. There is no need to compose clumsy Chinese verse and invite being laughed at as a silly show-off!" [2]

During this period, then, Japanese sinologues engrossed themselves almost entirely in what to them were the intensely serious and consequential concerns of morality and social order, with only a secondary interest in Chinese metaphysics and almost none at all in pure literature. Though they no doubt read and savored the great Chinese poets in moments of leisure, and on occasion wrote modest verses of their own in Chinese, only a few rare eccentrics such as the recluse Ishikawa Jōzan (1583–1672) dreamed of devoting their entire energies to the study and writing of poetry in Chinese. For the remainder of the Tokugawa period, the history of the *kanshi* is in effect the story of the gradual liberation of the form from its subservience to scholarship and morality and the recognition of its right to exist side by side with native poetic forms as a significant vehicle for aesthetic expression.

Before this could be accomplished, of course, it was first necessary to overcome the suspicions and animadversions of the Confucian scholars regarding the validity of literature itself. Most instrumental in bringing this about was the brilliant scholar and teacher Ogyū Sorai (1666–1728), whose influence initiated a new era in *kanshi* writing. Sorai went much farther than any of his predecessors in the Tokugawa period in his unquestioning adulation of Chinese culture, including its poetry, and actively encouraged the writing of *kanshi* among his students, partly as a means of attaining greater understanding and mastery of the Chinese language. Earlier Tokugawa sinologues, when they interested themselves in the subject at all, had tended

2. *Sentetsu sōdan kan* 4, biography of Kaibara Ekken, quoted from Ekken's *Shinshiroku*.

6

to be fairly eclectic in their literary tastes, approving the best poetry of T'ang, Sung, Yuan, and Ming times without pronounced partiality for any period. Sorai, on the other hand, avidly embraced the views of those Ming critics of the sixteenth century who advocated a return to the language and style of the past. Known as the *Ko-t'iao* or *Kakuchō* school, which might be translated as "formalists," they laid great stress upon the diction and formal elements of the poem, and advocated a careful imitation of the masterpieces of the past, which in the case of poetry for them meant in particular the works of the High T'ang, the period of Wang Wei, Li Po, and Tu Fu.

In terms of the *kanshi*, the results of Sorai's espousal of such views were on the whole disappointing. For one thing, the landscape of T'ang poetry, with its vast plains, windswept northern deserts, giant rivers, and colorfully cosmopolitan cities, was wholly different in scale and tone from anything to be found in Tokugawa Japan. Similarly, the experiences endured by the High T'ang poets, when a court of unparalleled luxury and splendor was suddenly imperilled and almost wiped out by internal revolt and foreign invasion and the nation plunged into discord and misery, were scarcely even imaginable to men living under the aegis of Tokugawa peace and social order.

Moreover, Sorai and his disciples were often imitating not T'ang poetry itself, but the imitations of it produced by the Ming archaizers, dull affairs at best, and the results are as a consequence doubly derivitive and barren. An anthology of Tokugawa *kanshi* that aimed to represent all periods and schools would perforce have to include examples of their work, no matter how uninteresting. My own selection makes no such pretense at comprehensiveness, and I have therefore for the most part passed them over in silence.

All critics, including those living at the time, agree that a profound change occurred in the world of *kanshi* poetry toward the close of the eighteenth century, though there is much disparity of opinion concerning just when it began and how rapidly it progressed. By this time most of Sorai's major poet-disciples had passed from the scene, and perhaps the age was ripe for reaction, though the question of the precise impetus and historical inevitability of sudden shifts in artistic taste must always remain something of a mystery. Certainly in the intellectual climate of the country as a whole there was a tendency to turn away from Confucianism in favor of the study of the native past or of "Dutch learning," the science and technology of the West as it filtered into Japan through the Dutch trading office in Nagasaki. The government itself helped to inhibit creativity in the field of Confucian studies by issuing prohibitions against the teaching of anything but the orthodox Chu Hsi philosophy in the officially sponsored schools.

One might expect that this would lead to an abandoning of interest in Chinese poetry and *kanshi* as well, a final shuffling off of the coil of sinophilia. Surprisingly, quite the opposite occurred. Instead, the *kanshi* broke free from its previous alliance with Confucian studies, always an uneasy marriage at best, and gained recognition as a full-fledged literary form in its own right. Men appeared who devoted their entire efforts to *kanshi* writing, professional poets who no longer felt it necessary to pose in Confucian garb, while many actual Confucian scholars, bereft of students by the changing times, gratefully turned to the teaching of poetry for the revenues it insured. Poetry societies and schools devoted to the teaching of *kanshi* writing proliferated, *shiwa* or collections of anecdotes and critical comments on the *kanshi* appeared in increasing numbers, and the *kanshi* soon came to rival native verse forms such as the *tanka* and *haiku* in the literary excitement it generated and the widespread popularity it enjoyed.

A key figure in the new movement, not as a poet but as a critic, was Yamamoto Hokuzan (1752–1812), who published spirited attacks on Sorai's followers and the theories they espoused. He himself embraced the ideals of a rival school of poetic theory that had arisen in late Ming times known as the *Hsing-ling* or *Seirei* school, which stressed the "spirit" (*seirei*) or inner feeling of the poem over formal considerations and encouraged individuality and innovation in subject. Though not necessarily denying the worth of T'ang poetry, it found the highest embodiment of its ideals in the works of the Sung, particularly those of Su Tung-p'o.[3] Hokuzan likewise enthusiastically endorsed Sung poetry, which Sorai and his group had largely rejected, and helped popularize it by supervising the publication of selections from three outstanding poets of the Southern Sung, Lu Yu, Fan Ch'eng-ta, and Yang Wan-li.

The effects of Hokuzan's new movement were surprisingly salutary. T'ang poetry, for all its occasional setting, pulls almost always in the direction of the timeless, the mythic, the grand and tragic gesture. But, as a glance at the native poetry will confirm, such grandiose and generalizing tendencies are basically inconsonant with the gist of Japanese literary taste. With the particularism and unpretentiousness of Sung poetry—what Kenneth Rexroth in speaking of the Sung poet Lu Yu calls its "ambiance of normalcy"—the Japanese could, however, feel quite at home, especially when such qualities coincided with, and perhaps in fact helped to foster, similar trends in the *tanka* and *haiku* poetry of the time. Thus the *kanshi* poets, freed from the obligation of constructing works on a scale appropriate to a vast continental nation—of, for example, depicting the modest

3. The views of the *Seirei* school had earlier been introduced to the Japanese priest Gensei (1623–1668) by the Chinese émigré to Japan Ch'en Yüan-yin (1587–1671) and are reflected in the two works by Gensei in my selection.

Sumida River as though it were the lordly Yangtze—could concentrate upon capturing the actual scenes and events around them. They wrote for a readership who had a sound knowledge of classical Chinese language and literature but no possibility of experiencing Chinese life at first hand. Such readers were no longer amused by the stiltedly sinicized landscapes of Sorai and his followers, in which familiar Japanese place names disappeared behind ponderous Chinese equivalents. They wanted to see their own landscape portrayed in the Chinese medium.

The first *kanshi* poets to take up this task and to attempt to apply the spirit of Sung poetry to Japanese themes were Rokunyo (sometimes read Rikunyo, 1734–1801), a priest of the Tendai sect, and Kan Sazan (1748–1827), a Confucian scholar and teacher in the province of Bingo in present-day Hiroshima Prefecture. Their poetry is distinguished by sincerity, homey realism, and a determination to deal with the daily scenes around them, and it is with their works that my selection begins in earnest.

These trends, and the taste for Sung poetry, continued to grow in importance until they completely dominated the *kanshi* scene. In time critics came forth to decry what they regarded as an inordinate enthusiasm for Sung poetry, and the shallowness of much of the work it inspired, and called for a more catholic approach, at the same time introducing new critical theories from Ch'ing China. Eventually a kind of eclecticism evolved, poets drawing for inspiration on whatever periods of Chinese literature or critical schools they found most congenial to their individual tastes, though the *kanshi* continued as before to be fairly simple and unaffected in language and predominantly realistic in tone. Rai San'yō (1780–1832), perhaps the greatest of the late Tokugawa *kanshi* poets and the one whose works are most voluminously represented in my selection, thus took for his models

T'ang, Sung, Ming, and even Ch'ing poets, evincing himself a master of many disparate styles and moods. The Zen monk Ryōkan (1758–1831), the other most important poet in my selection, stands in magnificent isolation from all contemporary schools and poetic theories, drawing inspiration from the eccentric T'ang Buddhist poet Han-shan and writing poetry that blithely ignores many of the technical dictates of traditional Chinese verse.

The fact is that by late Tokugawa times the Japanese had succeeded in naturalizing the medium of Chinese poetry and adapting it to their particular tastes and requirements to a degree never before realized in their history. The results were sometimes trite, even tasteless, though not without a certain wit and incongruous humor. Thus a category of verse known as *kyōshi* or "crazy poems" came into vogue, derived from Chinese and Gozan precedents and devoted to social satire, plays on words, or such quaint subjects as farting, shitting, fleas, the itch, etc.[4] The *kyōshi* thus stand in the same relation to serious *kanshi* as the *senryū* or humorous Japanese verses in 5-7-5 syllable form stand to the *haiku*. The following example by a man known only as Sūkatan, who seems to have flourished in the early nineteenth century, will serve as an illustration:

> Part of the roof blown away, rain pouring in,
> I crouch down, hastily squeeze into a corner of the closet.
> The children in a low voice query their father:
> "Is the bill collector coming again tonight?"

Another type of *kanshi* that, again with Chinese precedents, enjoyed wide popularity was the *chikushi* or "bamboo branch," a

4. For examples of *kyōshi* by the famous Gozan monk Ikkyū (1394–1481), see Donald Keene, "The Portrait of Ikkyū," *Landscapes and Portraits: Appreciations of Japanese Culture* (Tokyo: Kodansha International, 1971), pp. 226–41.

11

brief genre poem that customarily depicts scenes in the prostitute quarter. (See examples on p. 52.)

But while some poets were exploiting the *kanshi* form for mere displays of wit and frivolity, others were employing it for highly serious pronouncements. In the introduction to my earlier volume I discussed the potential advantages which the *kanshi*, because of its unrestricted length, offered for extended passages of description or for the treatment of philosophical, social, or political themes that could not, or by convention would not, be dealt with in native Japanese poetry. Many Tokugawa *kanshi* poets gratefully availed themselves of these possibilities for freedom of length and subject. Thus, to take some examples at random, Dazai Shundai's (1680–1747) verses on currency and rice prices, Yokoi Shōnan's (1809–1869) attacks on the principle of hereditary rule, or Hirose Kyokusō's (1807–1863) 290-line description of a smallpox epidemic, are all representative of poems that could not possibly have been encompassed in the Japanese verse of the time.

And, more importantly, when sentiments of loyalty to the imperial house and opposition to the shogunate began to stir and swell in late Tokugawa times, to be followed later by impassioned calls for the expulsion of the foreign traders, it was the *kanshi* that served most frequently and eloquently as the vehicle for their expression. It, rather than native Japanese verse, spread the word of protest and alarm and roused the patriotic ardor of the young, as numerous examples in my selection will attest. Thus the *kanshi*, far from being a mere literary appendage, as in certain periods of the past, became one of the most potent and influential mediums of expression in the intellectual world of the time.

The *kanshi* poets of the Tokugawa era were, like all their countrymen, forbidden by law to leave Japan and hence had no personal knowledge of China. Moreover, as we have seen, their works at times developed in certain peculiarly Japanese directions. This does not mean, however, that they were indifferent to contemporary Chinese literature or unconcerned with what Chinese readers might think of their writings.

In the early years of the Tokugawa there were a few learned Chinese residing in Japan, such as the Ming loyalists Ch'en Yüan-yün (1587–1671) and Chu Shun-shui (1600–1682) or the Zen monk Yin-yüan (1592–1673), founder of the Ōbaku branch of Zen, who might be consulted on matters of poetry. But for the most part the only Chinese the Japanese could contact in person were the merchants who resided in Nagasaki or came periodically in trading ships from the contintent. Through them the Japanese received quantities of Chinese books, including the latest works of poetry, fiction, and drama, which allowed them to keep fairly well abreast of literary developments on the continent, though inevitably a certain time lag was involved. The more enterprising sinologues went to Nagasaki and applied to the merchants or interpreters for instruction in spoken Chinese, though it is unlikely that such men had the background necessary to give authoritative critical opinions on the *kanshi*. The Japanese could also on occasion consult with Korean envoys and solicit their opinion, since Koreans of the educated class were quite at home in the Chinese language and employed it for much of their own literature.

But it is natural that the Japanese should have longed for some hint of interest, some nod of approval from the Chinese themselves. A copy of the poetic works of Arai Hakuseki (1657–1725), one of the most accomplished writers of the second period of Tokugawa *kanshi*, somehow reached China by way of the Ryukyus, where a Hanlin scholar named Cheng Jen-yüeh (*chin-shih* 1706) wrote a highly laudatory preface. When the book and preface in time made its way back to Hakuseki, he received it with understandable delight.[5] Another scholar and *kanshi* writer, Takashina Yōkoku (1719–1766), much encouraged by the abundant praise bestowed on his works by the Chinese merchants of Nagasaki, sent a letter with some of his poems by way of them to the eminent Ch'ing poet and critic Shen Te-ch'ien (1673–1769) asking for his appraisal. Shen duly recorded receipt of the gift in his journal under the year 1758, adding, "The man is not insincere in his intentions, but it is not proper that we should be exchanging letters back and forth with barbarians overseas, and so I have not answered him." [6]

Shen's remark suggests what the attitude of most Chinese must have been toward the *kanshi*, if indeed they were even aware of their existence. It was not until the late nineteenth century that anyone in China took serious notice of the Japanese works. The Ch'ing scholar Yü Yüeh (1821–1907), drawing on material sent to him by the Japanese newspaper editor Kishida Ginkō (1833–1905), compiled a selection of *kanshi* by Tokugawa poets, the *Tung-ying shih-hsüan* (published in 1883), along with a brief supplementary volume of biographical notes, the *Tung-ying shih-chi*, bestowing warm, even lavish praise on many of the poets. It came, however, at a time when most of them were no longer alive to appreciate it.

5. Yoshikawa Kōjirō, who has succeeded in discovering something of Cheng's identity, opines that Cheng praised Hakuseki's work with particular warmth because it adhered to the ideals of the Ming *Ko-t'iao* or archaic school which Cheng favored but which had by this time gone out of fashion in China. Yoshikawa Kōjirō, *Hōchō fushi* (Tokyo: Shinchōsha, 1971), pp. 81–193.

6. *Sentetsu sōdan kōhen kan* 5 and *Shen Kuei-yü tzu-ting nien-p'u* under Ch'ien-lung 23. Shen means, of course, that since China and Japan maintain no official diplomatic relations, it is not proper for private citizens of the two countries to exchange letters.

This rather sad story of cultural exchange, or the lack of it, points up one important fact. The Japanese in many periods of their history, particularly the Tokugawa, took a vital interest in the literature of a foreign country, namely China, and did their best to follow its development closely. Moreover, they went a step further and composed works of poetry and prose in the actual language of the country they admired. If the results are necessarily uneven, it is apparent that the practice helped greatly to enrich their native literature and to inculcate in them the habit of looking abroad for new sources of literary inspiration, new forms, and new critical theories. This is indubitably one of the main reasons why the Japanese were able to respond with such alacrity to the literature of the West when it was introduced to their country in Meiji times and to adapt it so quickly and effectively to their own uses. In this respect they stand in striking contrast to the Chinese, who have always been impeded in their appreciation of foreign cultures by their age-old ethnocentricity and towering sense of their own greatness.

As I have remarked, a prodigious amount of research remains to be done before we can hope to delineate with confidence and in detail the history of the Tokugawa *kanshi*. Many of the poetic works have never been reprinted in modern form, but exist only in rare old wood-block editions molding away in libraries, and what unknown manuscripts from the period may be hidden in family storehouses we can only guess. Thus the world of the Tokugawa *kanshi* remains at best a very roughly charted territory, one in which intensive efforts at exploration have only recently begun. Nevertheless, we know more about the overall development of Tokugawa *kanshi* than we do about that of the succeeding Meiji era (1868–1911), which in terms of *kanshi* history is a virtual wilderness.

The enthusiasm for *kanshi* writing that marked the late years of the Tokugawa era continued unabated into the Meiji, which began in 1868 with the abolition of the shogunate and the restoration of power to the emperor. As we have seen, the *kanshi* was the principal means of artistic expression for the scholars and patriots who led the movement to bring about the restoration, many of them sacrificing their lives for the cause, and their works were avidly read in early Meiji times, though perhaps more for ideological than for aesthetic reasons. Moreover, nearly all the prominent Meiji statesmen, military leaders, scholars, and men of letters were capable of writing *kanshi* and employed the form to give expression to their ideas and emotions, thus at times giving it a tone of high moral seriousness and didacticism it had not often known in later Tokugawa times. Schools teaching the writing of *kanshi* and *kanshi* societies flourished, modern printing methods encouraged the dissemination of collections of poetry and works on poetic criticism, and the leading newspapers regularly ran *kanshi* columns alongside those devoted to *haiku* and *tanka* poetry. Finally, the opening of the country allowed Chinese scholars to come to Japan or Japanese to journey to the continent to study under native teachers of Chinese verse, factors that helped to foster the spread and improvement of *kanshi* writing.

We customarily think of the Meiji as a time when the Japanese were entirely engrossed in the exploration of Western literature or the reforming and revitalization of their native forms of fiction, poetry, and drama, and it is therefore difficult to conceive of the amount of energy and enthusiasm that still went into the writing and appreciation of *kanshi*, particularly when Japanese literary historians themselves have so overwhelmingly ignored the subject. Yet, to cite merely a single example that comes to mind, one may recall how the protagonist of Mori Ōgai's *Vita Sexualis* and his friend Eiichi, schoolboys of fourteen, devoured the works of the contemporary *kanshi* poet Kikuchi

Sankei (1819–1891), though a glance at Sankei's poetry today would make one wonder how the boys could have found it such exciting fare. Seidensticker in his study of Nagai Kafū has noted Kafū's fondness for the *kanshi* poets, among them Narushima Ryūhoku (1837–1884), who is represented in my selection, though this is perhaps not so surprising in view of Kafū's well-known nostalgia for the past. More surprising will perhaps be the fact that my selection includes *kanshi* by two of the literary giants of the Meiji, men whose names customarily evoke anything but associations with Chinese verse, the *haiku* poet and literary reformer Masaoka Shiki (1867–1902), and the novelist and scholar of English literature Natsume Sōseki (1867–1916), the latter one of the most original *kanshi* poets of modern times.

Moreover, in this era when the Japanese were busy familiarizing themselves with Western literature and passing along what they had learned to the Chinese, the *kanshi* poets and teachers came to play a quite unexpected role in the opposite process, the introduction of Eastern literature, particularly Chinese poetry, to the West. Mori Kainan (1863–1911), the son of a famous *kanshi* poet and himself a writer of exegetical works on Chinese poetry, acted as teacher of *kanshi* and Chinese verse to the American scholar Ernest Fenollosa, and Fenollosa's notes on the subject, as everyone knows, formed the basis of Ezra Pound's highly influential *Cathay* translations and remarks on Chinese poetry. In addition, Kainan's written works guided another famous translator, Arthur Waley, in his initial explorations of the subject. Thus the first serious awareness of Chinese poetry came to the world of English letters to a large extent by way of the Japanese *kanshi* experts of the Meiji.

These remarks, sketchy as they are, will perhaps suggest how important the *kanshi* form remained in Meiji times and how intertwined it is with the development of other literary forms.

Since Japanese scholars have yet to write extensively on the subject, I do not feel confident to venture beyond this brief assessment, nor is my selection in any way an adequate coverage of the era. I have tried to include some of the most famous pieces, such as the succinct and poignant meditation by General Nogi, commander of the Japanese forces in the Russo-Japanese War, on the terrible price of victory, or "The White Tiger Battalion" (*Byakkotai*), a *kanshi* equivalent both in theme and popularity of "The Charge of the Light Brigade" and a favorite with performers of *shigin*, the special type of chanting used for public recitation of the *kanshi*. With Japanese of the period traveling freely to foreign countries, opportunities arose to apply the *kanshi* medium to wholly new themes and landscapes, resulting in works such as Narushima Ryūhoku's description of Niagara Falls, or the account of the battle of the Alamo by the geographer and world traveler Shiga Shigetaka (1863–1927), the latter incised in beautiful characters on a stone in the Alamo garden, where it is often eyed with curiosity but seldom read. My selection concludes with a *kanshi* on the atom bomb.

To all appearances, *kanshi* writing in Japan today is a dying art, practiced mainly by scholars of Chinese and by Buddhist priests, the two groups still likely to have sufficient command of Chinese to do so, though manuals on how to compose *kanshi* continue to be published. What has brought about its decline would seem to be no inevitable process of decay or flaw in the form itself, for, theoretically at least, it ought to have been susceptible to the same kind of reform and rejuvenation that restored vitality to native verse forms such as the *haiku* and *tanka*. What doomed it was the change in the Japanese educational system, which shifted emphasis from the study of classical Chinese to that of Western languages, especially English. This is particularly true since the Pacific War, when Chinese ceased to be a required subject in the public schools. In the last few years, however, there has begun to be a certain tentative questioning of this inordinate and at times seemingly pointless devotion to the study of English in the educational system and, perhaps with some stimulus from the continent, Chinese studies may yet begin to enjoy a revival of interest. The *kanshi*, with its continuously fluctuating history of alternate popularity and neglect in the past, may in fact turn out not to be dead at all but merely dormant.

BIBLIOGRAPHICAL NOTE

My selection consists of 135 poems in *shih* form and four prose pieces ranging in date from the fourteenth to the twentieth century, though the vast majority belongs to the years from around 1780 to 1916. Most of the poets are represented by only one or two works and biographical information has accordingly been kept to the minimum required to appreciate the poems themselves. These works, arranged in rough chronological order, are found in Part 1 of the book. Three writers who seem to me to be of particular interest—Ryōkan, Rai San'yō, and Natsume Sōseki—are represented by sizable selections of poetry and, in the case of the latter two, prose, each prefaced by an introductory essay. Their works constitute Part 2, Part 3, and Part 4 of the book respectively.

A few of the translations in my selection appeared originally in the *Anthology of Japanese Literature* (New York: Grove Press, 1955), and *Modern Japanese Literature* (Grove Press, 1956), both compiled and edited by Donald Keene, and in *Antioch Review* and *Montemora*. They are reproduced here with minor revisions. Most of the translations of Natsume Sōseki's *kanshi* are taken from a longer selection prepared at the request of the Japanese National Commission for UNESCO and published by the Japan Society for the Promotion of Science in Tokyo in 1972 in a volume entitled *Essays on Natsume Sōseki's Works*. I wish here to express my warm thanks to the East Asian Institute of Columbia University for a grant that assisted me in preparing the Meiji portions of this volume. The volume is dedicated to Matsushita Tadashi, a leading authority on *kanshi* history and former Professor of *Kambun* at Wakayama Daigaku. In 1954 I had an opportunity to study under him for a time, and he guided me in my first attempts to read and translate *kanshi*. Since then I have had countless occasions to be grateful for his invaluable assistance and warm friendship.

Because the amount of *kanshi* and *kambun* preserved from the period covered in this volume is so vast, I have had in many cases to rely upon anthologies in making my selection. Below are listed the principal anthologies and commentaries to which I am indebted:

Bokusetsuroku, in *Natsume Sōseki zenshū* 9. Tokyo: Chikuma shobō, 1971.

Fujikawa Hideo. *Edo kōki no shijintachi*. Tokyo: Mugi shobō, 1966.

Harada Ken'yū. *Nihon kanshi-sen*. Kyoto: Jimbun shoin, 1974.

Iguchi Atsushi. *Nihon kanshi*. 2 vols. Shin'yaku kambun taikei #45. Tokyo: Meiji shoin, 1972.

Kanno Dōmei, *Wa-Kan meishi ruisen hyōshaku*. Tokyo: Meiji shoin, rev. ed. 1956.

Kitamura Sawakichi. *Gozan bungaku shikō*. Tokyo: Fuzambō, 1941.

Matsushita Tadashi. *Edo jidai no shifū shiron: Min, Shin no shiron to sono sesshu*. Tokyo: Meiji shoin, 1969.

Meika shishū. Tsukamoto Tetsuzō, ed. Yūhōdō bunko, Tokyo: Yūhōdō shoten, 1918.

Rai San'yō shū. Dai-Nihon shisō zenshū kankōkai. Tokyo: Senshinsha, 1931.

Rai Seiichi & Itō Kichizō. *Rai San'yō shishō*. Iwanami bunko 3337–39. Tokyo: Iwanami shoten, 1944.

Tōgō Toyoharu. *Zenshaku Ryōkan shishū*. Osaka: Sōgensha, 1962.

Watanabe Hideei. *Ryōkan shishū*. Tokyo: Mokujisha, 1974.

Yamagishi Tokuhei. *Gozan bungaku-shū, Edo kanshi-shū*. Nihon koten bungaku taikei #89. Tokyo: Iwanami shoten, 1966.

Yoshikawa Kōjirō. *Sōseki shichū*. Iwanami shinsho #640. Tokyo: Iwanami shoten, 1967.

Part 1

WORKS FROM THE FOURTEENTH CENTURY
TO THE PRESENT

KOKAN SHIREN (1278–1346)

(A Kyoto Zen monk, scholar, and representative of early *Gozan bungaku*.)

✍ *Autumn Day Stroll in the Country*

Shallow water, soft sand,
    one path that angles along;
the clack of a loom, murmur of a grove—
    people living there.
Beyond banked clouds of yellow,
    white waves rise up:
fragrant stalks of rice ripening,
    bounded in buckwheat blossom.

✍ Earthquake

Still things moving,
     firm become unfirm,
land like ocean waves,
     house like a boat—
a time to be fearful,
     but to delight as well:
no wind, yet the wind-bells
     keep on ringing.

✍ On Something Observed

Torn remains of a cobweb,
     one strand dangling down—
a stray petal fluttering by
     has been tangled, caught in its skein,
all day to dance and turn,
     never once resting—
elsewhere in my garden,
     no breeze stirs.

CHŪGAN ENGETSU (1300–1375)

(A Zen monk who visited Yuan China.)

🖎 Spring Snow

Shinshi (1341), second month, twenty-fifth day,
springtime blizzard, snow piled five feet deep!
I first heard it scrabbling crablike by the window,
was suddenly startled by treetop winds whistling and lashing;
then the lashing turned to a rumble-roaring sound,
a thousand thunders contending, buffeting each other.
From open windows I peered dimly at tons of white ash,
hurried to close the shutters, pile up the mats.
Bamboos planted last year abruptly snapped in two,
trees bent and broken—no time to worry now.
Kamakura city by the southeast sea—
oldsters tell me they've witnessed nothing like this.
Ever since the start of spring this year
Heaven has sent such snows as are seldom seen.
Muck and mud on paths sink the oxen to their hams,
old friends coming to see me can barely pick a way through.
Travelers from up north, used to this, know how to
    sponge from others,
but local folk, hesitant-hearted, don't dare beg for help.
Neighborhoods only steps apart hardly call on one another,
merchants all doze the day through, commerce completely cut
    off.
Rich families, stocked for winter, have more than enough on
    hand,

trays and stands strung out with surfeit of dried and salted
  meats.
Within their gold-flecked curtains, what do they know of the
  cold,
sipping wine, singing softly, enjoying themselves to the full?
But in poor homes days on end no smoke from the chimney,
the lean lying in wretched houserows, as though in their grave.
Ten thousand scrolls of writing useless to fill a belly,
never will they heal the morning's hunger and ache.
One bundle of kindling costs higher than the sky,
five cups of stale yellow rice nowhere to be bought.
Some say, late as it is, the snow omens good harvests,
but for me it means no escape from a brawling of sword and
  spear.[1]

1. Because of the riots that will result from the shortage of supplies?

☙ Atami

(A rare view of the famous hot spring resort near Kamakura as it was in the fourteenth century, with a glimpse of the island of Hatsushima in the distance.)

Midnight dreams broken by the hissing roar—
hot water boiling from the roots of the cliff;
pipes this way and that lead the water, houses wreathed in
    steam,
every inn fitted with a bath, rooms let out to travelers.
By the sea's border land is warm—winter it never snows,
though cold days on mountain paths, one treads through
    frost at dawn.
A far-off island in fine rain, black with clouds and fog;
over red tides I watch the moon sink dimly out of sight.

PRIEST GENSEI (1623–1668)

🖎 *Autumn, a Visit to the Byōdō-in Temple*

(The Byōdō-in in Uji south of Kyoto, built in 1052 and a well-known tourist attraction, appears to have been in a state of considerable neglect in Gensei's time. Situated beside the Uji River, it fronts on a pond, called in the poem "merit-giving" because of the charitable nature of Buddhist institutions. The sutra inscription on the panel on the south wall was formerly believed to be from the hand of Minamoto no Shumbō, though now it is generally attributed to Fujiwara no Kaneyuki. The central image is a gilded statue of the Buddha Amida by the famous sculptor Jōchō (d. 1057). Minamoto no Takakuni (1004–1077), better known by the title Uji Dainagon, had a summer retreat near the temple called Nansen-in or Cloister of the Southern Springs. The poet was a priest of the Nichiren sect.)

Forest trees stripped in autumn, an ancient Buddhist temple,
where mists from the waters are deepest, dark even in daytime.
The magnificent hall weathered, red and green paint peeled off;
the pond meant to bring merit gone dry, only lotuses left.
On the silver-leafed panel still remaining, Shumbō's writing;
the golden countenance untouched by time, Jōchō's handi-
　　work.
The old Cloister of the Southern Springs—where is it now?
Not a soul passing this way, evening winds are chill.

Hut: Thinking of a Friend. My friend had not come to see me for a long time, and because I was ill I couldn't go to pay a visit. In longing, I wrote this poem.

(The language of the poem recalls the ancient Chinese folksongs of the *Book of Odes*.)

I waited for you in my hut, I did—
silent, silent, feeling little joy,
but today again the sun is setting.

I waited for you by the gate, I did—
silent, silent, not speaking a word,
but today again twilight's coming on.

I waited for you along the road, I did—
silent, silent, walking alone,
but today again the darkness begins to fall.

🖉 *Visiting Ichijō-ji: ninth month, third day, 1697*

(Ichijō-ji in Jinsai's time was a peaceful country village at the foot of Mount Hiei northeast of Kyoto. Like so many people who think of retiring to a house in the country, Jinsai, an eminent Confucian scholar, never got beyond the stage of thinking, and died eight years later in his home in Kyoto.)

Amid a vastness of autumn colors I climb the slopes,
clouds filtering through old trees, first of the wild geese
      winging.
In country gardens persimmons are ripe; crows make off with
      them in their beaks;
in stream valleys lots of mushrooms; people lug them home
      on their backs.
So far from the city, I see no gritty whirls of dust,
only where forests are deep, the trailing, tumbling mists.
Another day, should I be looking for a place to live,
these meadow stream banks at the foot of Mount Hiei!

ITŌ TŌGAI (1670–1736)

✍ *Impressions of the Countryside*

Low hedges bent by the wind, festooned in morning glories;
old roofs steamy with rain, sprouting fungus ears—
at door on door, bright lamps hurry the evening chores;
in village after village, noisy drums give thanks
　　for autumn bounty.

TANI ROKKOKU (1729–1809)

✍ Strolling in a Nearby Village

Water flushed into paddies,
    water flooding the ditches;
by edges of the ditch streams
    water-striders [1] drift.
Water-striders drift and skim—
    just like me
skating back and forth how many times,
    how many times stopping to rest?

1. *Mizusumashi*, variously called in English water-striders or whirligig beetles, small, delicate-legged insects that skate over the surface of the water. The poet was the father of the well-known painter Tani Bun-chō.

✍ The Cowherd

At the foot of the bank, many fragrant grasses;
at the top of the bank, many trailing willows;
trailing willows mingling to make fine shade,
dense canopies that shut out the glare of the sky.
The herdboy rests beneath them,
breeze blowing cool under his bamboo-grass hat.
The old cow, sated, stares blankly around,
little calf never leaves her side.
The herdboy splashes water, washing off the mud,
breaks a branch to switch away mosquitoes and horse-flies,
lies down, pillowing his head on a riverbank stone;
he and the cow have forgotten each other.
Startled from his one dream by a distant bell,
every hill enveloped in evening sun,
leisurely he rides the cow's back,
on the road home the long-drawn notes of his flute.

✍ *Early Summer, Paying a Second Visit to the Kankantei of the Kanshō-in in the Tōei.*

(Tōei is another name for the famous Kan'ei-ji, a Buddhist temple in Ueno in Edo. The poet, a priest of the Tendai sect, had obviously paid an earlier visit to the temple when its renowned cherry trees were in bloom.)

I recall that former splendid party,
    drunk with the scent of flowers;
I come again to find the green
    of new foliage thick about the doors.
Pale sunlight, gentle breeze,
    and beyond the little verandah
dandelions, grown old,
    send balls of fluff flying.

✍ Frosty Dawn

I wake from my dawn pillow,
    frost half dried;
clear sunlight fills the window,
    already a faint warmth—
lying, I watch as cold flies
    gather on the shoji,
rubbing their legs together,
    falling off, flying up again.

✍ Morning-glories

By the well side,
　　　　morning-glories I transplanted,
wild tendrils climbing the rail,
　　　　angling this way and that:
before I know it the well rope's
　　　　been completely seized—
now I beg water
　　　　from the house next door.

The poem bears a striking resemblance to the famous *haiku* by Kaga no Chiyo (1703–1775):

Asagao ni　　　　By morning-glories
tsurube torarete　my well-bucket's been seized—
morai-mizu　　　borrowing water

In view of their respective dates, it is probable that Rokunyo took the idea from Chiyo. One can see how different is the effect created by the seventeen-syllable *haiku* and the twenty-eight-syllable *kanshi*. The custom of producing *kanshi* versions of Japanese poems dates back to the *Shinsen Man'yōshū*, a collection of *tanka* with *kanshi* paraphrases in seven-character *chüeh-chü* form compiled in the period 893–913 and attributed to Sugawara no Michizane.

✍ Early Autumn Evening

Bath over, on a chair
        I catch the evening cool,
earth in the garden, sprinkled and swept,
        making a good smell.
On the palm leaves
        soft rain falls;
the wax-papered lamp glows
        over the dark verandah

✍ *Written on the Ōi River*

(The poem describes the swift section of the Ōi River west of Kyoto as it flows through the Hozu Narrows. In 1606 the rapids were cleared of obstructions so that rafts could bring timber down from the wooded areas to the northwest.)

Clear current, craggy boulders,
    green rounding and curling,
schools and schools of ayu
    going off and back again—
suddenly a lumber raft
    threads down the narrows,
its light pole crinkling
    the mountains in the water.

KAN SAZAN (1748–1827)

✍ *On the Road to Takaya*

Mountain clouds half colored
     where setting sun streams through;
trees along the mounds, bleak and bare
     from tenth month frosts.[1]
At a country stall they urge me to rest,
     offer buckwheat and flour noodles,
a wicker tray of silver threads
     fetched up fragrant from the steamer.

1. The mounds are the so-called *ichiri-zuka*, tree-planted mounds along the roadside at intervals of one *ri* (2¼ miles). The poet was a Confucian scholar and teacher. Takaya, near his home, was in Bingo, present-day Hiroshima Prefecture.

⚞ Summer Day

Running from the rain,
      travelers crowd at the foot of the tree,
southern speech, northern dialect,
      noisy hubbub of laughter.
After a while, clouds scatter,
      sky darkening to night—
east, west, north, south—
      each hurries his separate way.

Winter Night, Reading Books

Snow hugs the mountain hall,
      tree shadows deepen;
wind-bell at the eaves hangs motionless,
      night waning away—
quietly I collect the scattered volumes,
      mulling over passages I didn't understand:
one spike of blue-flamed lamp,
      thoughts from a thousand years ago.

✍ Written on a Summer Night

Country clouds scatter four ways,
      night sharp and clear,
above my head the silver river
      seems to be speaking.
Neighbor children, hating to leave the cool,
      still not gone to bed,
finally come where I lean on my stick humming,
      asking the names of the stars.

Rainy Season

How many days of spring rain
        since I've seen the sun?
Yet I delight in the new pools
        that shine before my porch.
Last year the burning drought
        continued through the fall—
even in river towns I heard
        the water-seller's cry.

🖎 For My Younger Brother Shinkei on the Seventeenth Anniversary of His Death

I from the first was the bankside willow,
    waiting to be stripped by the cold;
you were the stalwart parasol tree,
    destined to flourish and endure.
Who'd have guessed I'd be the one
    making offerings to you—
how swift the stars and frosts
    of these seventeen years!

RAI KYŌHEI (1756–1834)

(He was the younger brother of Rai Shunsui and uncle of Rai San'yō. Diakon are the large white radishes, of which there are numerous varieties, so important in Japanese cuisine. Mihara and Satō are regions in the poet's native fief of Aki, present-day Hiroshima.)

Daikon Song

Have you seen
the daikon of Mihara, big around as a thigh,
to be boiled after frost-fall, sweeter than milk?
Or have you seen
the Satō variety, slim as fingers,
several feet when full grown, bland, but tasty too?
Each with its heaven-given nature, each offers its best;
what creature wins the world's praise for possessing all
        virtues at once?
The plump you cannot pass up, the thin too are good;
Flying Swallow, Jade Ring—who could despise either? [1]
The hundred vegetables, the hundred fishes all are thus—
our only regret—we lack a master chef to prepare them!

---

1. Flying Swallow, a favorite of Emperor Ch'eng of the Han, was noted for her slim waist and fragile beauty; Jade Ring is Yang Kuei-fei, concubine of Emperor Hsüan-tsung of the T'ang, famous as the epitome of the plump, round-faced beauty.

48

TATE RYŪWAN (1762–1844)

✍ *Playing Bowl-and-Bead*

("Bowl-and-bead" was the Edo period version of the shell game, played in the same way and designed to trick betters out of their money.)

Nothing under the bowl—it's shifted again!
In all this turning and overturning, who can tell
      truth from illusion?
But you needn't be so proud of your skill at palming—
lots of people nowadays can pull that kind of switch!

ŌKUBO SHIBUTSU (1767–1837)

✍ Sudden Shower

One assault of wild thunder, one assault of wind;
a confused rush of white rain battering blinds and lattice.
Bamboo shoots that poked up, green scattering half the garden;
blossoms fallen, red that filled the trellis gone.
Ant commander's headlong rout, ranks in total chaos;
butterfly envoy, whirling in alarm, mission hard to accomplish.
The only ones unconcerned, swallows who patch their nests,
delighted that mud in the roadway has suddenly turned soft.

✍ *Abandoned Garden*

Grass so deep you can no longer see the little old cottage;
wild bamboo growing in clumps where fledgling bush warblers
    hide.
And now dyers have come to take over the empty lot:
how many poles of indigo blue dangling in the new clear spell!

NAKAJIMA SŌIN (1780–1856)

(Writer of a very popular series of 120 seven-character *chüeh-chü* or quatrains on Kyoto entitled *Miscellaneous Songs of the Four Seasons East of the Kamo* (*Ōtō shiji zasshi*). Consisting mainly of *chikushi* or genre sketches of scenes in the Gion geisha quarter, the series served as a model for similar works on Osaka and Edo and influenced such Meiji Japanese language poets as Yosano Akiko and Yoshii Isamu. The following are two poems from the series.)

1. (A *maiko* or apprentice geisha escorts a customer across the Kamo River.)

No more light from second-story lamps,
    sounds of water rushing,
one sliver of waning moon
    brightening the stillness:
a thirteen-year-old girl
    with a customer she knows well
braves wind and dew
    to see him across the bridge.

2. (It was, and still is, the custom for Kyotoites to visit the Yasaka Shrine in Gion on New Year's Eve to pray for good fortune and receive a spark from the shrine fire with which to light their new year's cooking fires. In the poet's time it was also part of the proceedings for worshippers to shout curses at one another in the dark, thus ridding themselves of pent-up frustrations and insuring luck in the coming year.)

Before Gion Shrine, determined to drive away poverty,
citizens come in supplication, milling about till dawn.
As though to get rid of a whole year's vexations,
    they feign jeers and curses, striving to outshout each other.

TERAKADO SEIKEN (1796–1868)

(The author was an essayist and Confucian scholar; the following piece is a prose note appended to five poems on the beauty of hearing the *uguisu* or bush warbler singing on the opposite side of the Sumida River from his house in Edo.)

As a rule, the sounds of most things are pleasanter when heard from a distance. Certainly that's true of someone reciting from a book, beating on a wooden fish to keep time to a sutra, or playing a koto. The doves in the wood calling to the rain, the wild geese winging beneath the moon and warning of frost, are both delightful when heard a long way off. Woodwinds from a pleasure boat, flutes of the fisherman's craft, when far away have a resonance all their own. Temple bells, castle drums too are very fine if one is not too close by. Frogs that sound as though they were croaking at your pillowside make an intolerable racket, but if there is sufficient distance in between, they're well worth listening to. A dog's bark is basically ugly, but if the dog happens to be on the other side of the woods, the sound is rather pleasant, and the same can be said for the sound of a waterwheel. And when you're traveling through the mountains and hear such sounds, assuring you that there's a village ahead, they can be a source of delight. At such times one is overjoyed to hear them. A horse chomping away at his fodder—what possible attraction could such a sound have? And yet, if you are putting up for the night alone in some cold inn and such a sound comes to your ears from the other side of the wall, it is in fact distinctly agreeable. That's what Mr. Ch'ao meant when he wrote:

> Light rain, darkness all around,
> and I can't get to sleep;

53

> I lie and listen to the skinny horse
> > munching the last of his beanstalks.[1]

The call of the bush warbler is lovely even when it comes to your ears from close by. But when you hear it echoing from the far side of the river, you will discover in it a wholly different charm. Alas, however, it's not the kind of thing you can wrap up and send to your friends—that's my real regret!

1. The Sung poet Ch'ao Pu-chih (1053–1110), a disciple of Su Tung-p'o.

✍ Crier-to-Heaven

(*Chiao-t'ien-erh* or "crier-to-Heaven" is a Chinese name for the skylark. The poem, written in 1814, draws on Chinese mythology and is presumably an allegory.)

Crier-to-Heaven, crier-to-Heaven,
Heaven so high high up, you so low—
wheat field breezes gentle, spring balmy by now,
winging, winging, ringed in sound, you soar to Heaven's dome,
soar to Heaven's dome, reach the doors of Heaven;
but Heaven's doors are deep and awesome, tiger and leopard
    crouch there.
Hsi-ho lashes the sun, breaking her whip of fire;
Jade Maiden tosses arrows, thunder and lightning streak down.[1]
Ah—hard as you try, your efforts are vain—
who will listen to your tiny piping cry?
    Have you not heard how
the *luan* bird and the crane stand silent by jasper stairs
while fortune and safety descend to their sons and grandsons?

1. The goddess Hsi-ho is the charioteer of the sun; Jade Maiden, another goddess of Heaven, amuses herself with the ancient Chinese game of pitching arrows into a pot.

(The writer, a distinguished scholar and *kanshi* poet, in his late years became an ardent supporter of the *Sonnō-jōi* movement which advocated
restoration of power to the emperor and expulsion of the foreigners.
The following poem, an attack on the shogunate, is one of a series on
political themes written in 1858 and would probably have cost the
writer his life had he not conveniently died of cholera shortly after,
before the government had begun to take steps to suppress him and his
followers. Hence the popular saying at the time, Seigan was "good at
shi," which may mean either "good at poetry" or "good at dying.")

You, whose ancestors in the mighty days
roared at the skies and swept across the earth,
stand helpless now to drive off these wrangling foreigners—
how empty your title "Queller of Barbarians"!

YANAGAWA KŌRAN (1804–1879)

(The wife of Yanagawa Seigan; she studied the writing of *kanshi* under her husband, and it was generally supposed that he rewrote her works for her. After his death in 1858, however, she surprised the world by producing poetry that was even superior to her previous works.)

✍ Coming Home at Night in the Snow

The maid to help me, I pick my way home,
long ditches frozen over, third watch of the night,
my pair of light clogs in unresisting softness,
windy snow sharply slanting, the parasol full of its sound.

EMA SAIKŌ (1787–1861)

To Inscribe on My Portrait

(A student of Rai San'yō; on her "one mistake," see his poem on p. 152.)

Lonely room, fiddling with a brush as the years go by;
one mistake in a lifetime, not the kind to be mended.
This chaste purity to rejoice in—what do I resemble?
A hidden orchid, a rare bamboo—sketch me in some such cold form.

ŌZAKI BUNKI (19th cen.)

(She was a student of Yamamoto Hokuzan (1752–1812), though little else is known of her.)

✍ Night Thoughts

Crafty rats, tricking me forever, gnawing holes in the wall;
always alone in an empty bedroom, the nights like years.
I close the book by my pillow, prepare for dreams,
when the lamp, growing dimmer and dimmer, precedes me in
    sleep.

FUJII CHIKUGAI (1807–1866)

(A student of Rai San'yō; his works reflect the views of his teacher. The following poem expresses his reverence for the Southern Court of Emperor Go-Daigo, centered at Mt. Yoshino; see p. 133.)

✍ Yoshino

Pine and cypress by the old tomb
    howl in winds from the sky:
I came to the mountain temple looking for spring,
    found the loneliness where spring had been.
The old monk, eyebrows of snow,
    for a time puts down his broom,
where fallen blossoms are deep,
    talks of the Southern Court.

🖋 Viewing Nara from a Distance in Wind and Rain

(The pagodas are those of the Tōdai-ji and Kōfuku-ji. The poem expresses anger at the affluent position of Buddhism and the lack of reverence paid to the imperial family.)

Thrusting halfway up into the sky—the two pagodas;
still more temples peering down on the nine avenues of the city.
Twelve Imperial gravemounds, so low you can't even see
  them—
black wind, white rain fill the southern capital.

✍ Traveling down the Yodo River
   on a Winter Night

Quiet dreams interrupted,
    bits of hard metal poking me—
wild geese beating out the cold watches,
    water about to ice over.
I get up and raise the thin blind,
    moon not yet risen;
dark wind blows, fluttering
    the candle on my night boat.

TAKEUCHI UNTŌ (1815–1862)

✍ *Spending the Night in a Rundown Temple*

What a laugh—the priest is deaf,
    can't follow what I'm saying;
through the long long night,
    who'll keep me company?
Ragged clouds snare the moon,
    smudging it till it's black.
Big as a hawk, an old bat
    swoops out from the altar.

MURAKAMI BUSSAN (1810–1879)

✍ Long Ago

Long ago I traveled through Yamato,
from Mount Yoshino heading for Taima,
got confused in the mountains, lost the trail,
coming out of cherry blossoms, into blossoms again.
Steep ridges winding up to weird peaks,
not the barest trace of a house,
where could that sound be coming from,
a ting-ting drifting through vines and brush?
A cave in the cliff, and deep inside,
a man chanting the *Lotus Sutra*,
stiff and still as a withered tree,
hanging from his shoulders, the tattered robe of a monk,
the sea of his mind calm and clear—
how could the smallest wave ruffle it?
Politely as I could, I asked the way ahead;
laughing, he pointed to mists at the mouth of the ravine.
What a pity I didn't press him for the secret of his Zen—
even today I recall it with deep regret,
and when I find myself wrapped in clouds of wordly dust,
I remember that old hermit of the hills.

TOMOBAYASHI MITSUHIRA (1813–1864)

✍ *Written in the second month of 1861 when
I left the temple and returned to lay life.*

From the beginning I was a pure man of the land of the gods;
by mistake I became a slave to the Buddha, preaching Emptiness.
Now I abandon Buddha—may he hold me no grudge!
From the beginning I was a pure man of the land of the gods.

    My distant ancestors were priests of the Kumano Shrine.[1]
Along the way some forebear of mine in the Keichō era
(1596–1614) became a Buddhist priest, and since then our family
has continued in this occupation for thirteen generations. But I do
not believe in Buddha, a great realization which has just now come
over me. So this morning I will leave the temple. If my ancestors
have knowledge of what I am doing, I wonder if they will think me
filial or unfiial?[2]

1. The famous Shinto shrine in the Kii Peninsula.

2. The prose note appended to the poem is in Chinese like the poem;
the poet's family were followers of the Jōdo Shinshū sect, which per-
mits priests to marry and to pass the supervision of their temples on to
their sons. The poem, simple as it is, conveys the feeling of spiritual
unrest and questioning typical of the age. English readers may be familiar with it from the fact that it is quoted in Mishima Yukio's *Homba*,
translated by Michael Gallagher as *Runaway Horses*, p. 274 of the English translation. The writer was executed three years later for taking
part in an attempt to overthrow the shogunate.

SAKUMA SHŌZAN (1811–1864)

✍ *Song of History: Peter the Great*

He pushed back the eastern borders three thousand miles,
learned the Dutch science and taught it to his people.
Idly we sit talking of our long dead heroes—
in a hundred years have we bred such a man?

PRIEST GESSHŌ (1817–1858)

On Hearing that the Port of Shimoda Has Been Opened to the Foreigners

(Written early in 1855, the year after the shogunate had signed treaties with the United States and other Western powers opening the ports of Shimoda and Hakodate. The Shimoda area was devasted by earthquakes late in 1854. To many Japanese of this period the meat-eating Westerners were no more than reeking animals. The poet was a Buddhist priest of the Jōdo Shinshū sect.)

For seven miles by the river hills the dogs and sheep forage;
the hues of spring visit the wastes of quake-ridden earth.
Only the cherry blossoms take on no rank barbarian stench,
but breathe to the morning sun the fragrance of a nation's soul.

RAI MIKISABURŌ (1825–1859)

✍ Crossing Hakone Pass

(He was the youngest son of Rai San'yō. In 1843 he had crossed Hakone Pass on his way from Kyoto to Edo, where he enrolled as a student in the Shōheikō, the official school of the shogunate. Later he became active in the movement to overthrow the shogunate and restore power to the throne. He was arrested and sent to Edo early in 1859, crossing the pass in the kind of cramped cage used for transporting criminals. He was imprisoned and executed in the tenth month of the same year.)

That other time, spirits so high I seemed to soar over the clouds,
racing east on a fast horse, never even noticing mountains.
Today on an anxious road, spring rain cold,
a criminal's cage to rock my dreams, I cross Hakone Pass.

✒ In Prison

I wanted to drive back the clouds, with these hands sweep clear
      the evil stars,
but the ground gave way beneath my feet, I plunged to Edo
      Prison.
Idiot frogs fret at the bottom of their well;
the brilliance of the great moon falters on the horizon.[1]
I wait the death sentence, no news from home;
in dreams, the ring of swords: I slash at sea monsters.
When the wind and rain of many years have cloaked my stone
      in moss,
who will remember this mad man of Japan?

1. The frogs are the shortsighted statesmen of the shogunate, the moon is the powerless emperor in Kyoto.

FUJITA KOSHIRŌ (1842–1865)

⚘ *In the Army*

(The writer led an attempt at armed resistance against the shogunate but was apprehended and put to death.)

To fret at the times, bewail the age—how pointless!
More sense in howling at the moon or fashioning rhymes on
    flowers.
Should anyone come to camp and ask for me today,
say the General went to bed drunk and hasn't waked up yet.

⚰ The White Tiger Battalion

(The poem deals with a famous incident in the Boshin civil war of 1868, a struggle between the armies of the imperial government and the scattered forces that remained loyal to the Tokugawa shogunate. The lord of the fief of Aizu in northeast Japan was among the latter. His castle at Wakamatsu was known as Crane Castle. The Byakkotai or White Tiger Battalion was a group of boys aged fourteen to sixteen organized to defend the castle. Most were killed when the castle was attacked by government forces in the eighth month of 1868, but a group of nineteen managed to fight their way out of the castle and retreat to a hill to the north. Surrounded by the enemy and seeing smoke rising from the castle, they concluded that the cause was lost and committed suicide. The poet Sahara was a Confucian scholar and native of Wakamatsu. The following work has enjoyed great popularity, especially among devotees of *shigin* or *kanshi*-chanting, and is often recited to the accompaniment of a *kembu* or sword dance.)

Young men who banded together, the White Tiger Battalion;
while the nation walked in peril, they guarded the battlements.
The vast army came at them with a suddenness of wind and
    rain;
the grim breath of slaughter blackened the bright day.
War drums boomed a hundred peals of thunder;
as giant cannon belched volley on volley, the dead piled up
    in heaps.
Determined to die, they charged the ranks, hair stiff with rage,
fiercely slashing left and right till they'd cleared a path.
Tides of battle against them, they fought as they retreated,
bandaging cuts and wounds, gulping medicine to stay the pain.

Enemy to the fore and aft of them, which way could they go?
Leaning on swords, they followed hidden paths, climbed the
      crest of the hill.
South they saw Crane Castle, cannon fire and smoke ascending;
crying out in anguish, choking back tears, they paced
      back and forth.
"Shrines of our fief destroyed—our work is ended!"
Nineteen boys slashed their bellies, crumpled to the ground.
Since that time, ten and seven years have come and gone;
painting and prose have told their tale to the world.
Still the light of their fierce loyalty burns, as though
      only a day had passed,
outshining those heroes who died in the cause of T'ien Heng! [1]

1. T'ien Heng, lord of the feudal state of Ch'i in China, defied Kao-tsu,
the founder of the Han dynasty, and in 202 B.C. committed suicide
rather than submit to him. When T'ien Heng's five hundred followers
received the news, they too committed suicide. The allusion is particularly apt because both the White Tiger Battalion and T'ien Heng's followers died in a hopeless cause, defying rulers—Emperor Meiji in the
case of the former and Emperor Kao-tsu in the latter—who were des-
tined to become leaders of a unified nation.

OGASAWARA GOKYŌ (1822–1881)

✍ *Written after the Revolt*

(The poet was a scholar of the fief of Aizu, which, as we have seen, un-successfully resisted the imperial forces in the Boshin civil war in 1868.)

At dawn I gathered up the bones in the fields,
nights took shelter in a village in the fields,
village empty even of dogs and chickens,
sorrow in my heart I cannot describe:
my lord disgraced, yet I could not die for him;
my homeland destroyed, I could not save it.
Amid the grasses I seek to go on living,
shamefaced before those ghosts who've gone below.

YAGUCHI KENSAI (1817–1879)

End of Winter in a Mountain Village

(In 1872, the government changed from the lunar to the solar calendar, announcing that the third day of the twelfth lunar month of Meiji 5 should become the first day of the first solar month of Meiji 6 or 1873. It will be remembered that in China and Japan New Year was traditionally regarded as the beginning of spring.)

Suddenly they change the calendar, spring coming much earlier, but though they force New Year on us, it's not the real thing.
Autumn harvesting not yet over, there's no rice to eat;
this first month in a mountain village, no one gets drunk.

NARUSHIMA RYŪHOKU (1837–1884)

✍ *Aboard a Ship Leaving Yokohama*

Where is Mount Ararat,
where the wide wind-blown billows drowned the sky in blue?
In the hold of our ship ride cows, sheep, and pigs,
recalling a thousand autumns ago, that vessel of Noah's.

✎ Saigon

(The poet is looking at the Saigon River)

Heat of the night bears down, sleep easily broken:
white sand, green grass fill the riverbank before me.
In gardens of home, frost by now has already fallen;
I stare in wonder at these southern fireflies big as stars.

✍ Niagara Falls

The startled traveler wakes to the thunder by his pillow,
rises and climbs among old trees to the roaring brink:
in the deep night, heaven and earth one vista of white;
the moon comes, parting the mile-high curtain of pearls.

⍦ *Pronouncement on Returning Home*

No title, no lands—no worries either;
the Lord of Heaven allowed me to roam at will.
Do you know what joys are in the world of men,
on these two legs tramping the whole globe over?
Never mind the new frost that invades my temples;
high winds sigh—autumn in the old gardens of home.
The lovely women of Milan, Paris wine—
in my elation, who can I talk to of those journeys of the past?

PRIEST MOKURAI (1838–1911)

In India, Deeply Moved

(Written in 1873 when Shimaji Mokurai, a priest of the Jōdo Shinshū sect and an important religious leader of the time, visited Buddhist sites in India on his way home from a trip to Europe.)

That white whiteness—snowy mountain snow, cold in my eyes;
this surge surging—the flow of Ganges waters unending;
cold wind sighing sighing, a road ten thousand miles,
and now I turn my head, look back upon that distance,
recall how the sage cast his greatest treasures aside,
so many years bitter and sweet, searching for the bridge.[1]
Waves of his mercy wash us three thousand years away;
how many countless souls has he eased in birth and death!
Lifetimes have a limit, his mercy no end—
as I walk in his wondrous traces, all troubles are forgotten.
Train wheels shatter a traveler's moody dream—
outside Calcutta, the evening sun still glows.

1. Shakyamuni, the founder of Buddhism, a prince and heir to a throne, renounced all worldly goods and set out on a long search for a "bridge" or means to bring salvation to all beings.

✍ Airing Books

The brave hero prizes his sword, the beauty her mirror,
the doting scholar loves his books—books are life to him!
Airing books carefully, I caution the boy:
"See the dust is whisked away, chase out all the bugs!
Souls of ancient men are garnered in these words—
if we soil them, we court the ire of the dead!"
The boy replies, "You treasure these books, Master, but you
      never read them—
if there are souls in the books, I think they must weep!"

Song of Victory: the Battle of Port Arthur

With the King's million I struck the proud foe,
from the plains drove upon the fort till the dead piled in hills.
With this shame I must now face their fathers:
to our song of victory today, how many men return?

✍ Poor Man's Hut

(Shiki was the greatest *haiku* poet of the Meiji period and a leader in the movement to revitalize traditional Japanese poetry.)

Poor man's hut—still room for my knees,
shelf stacked with a hundred volumes;
on west wall an old painting hanging,
arhat with eyeballs lightning bright;
east wall, lines from the *Li sao*, [1]
a rainbow descending in blazoned hues;
straw raincoat, hat with old words written on it;
precious sword, memento of battles—
high hopes of youth bit by bit ground down,
I envy myself the wanderings I once had.
Cramped and cringing, I never go out the gate,
thinking only how the rounding years go by.
Bamboo breath—congelation of green cloud;
plum blossoms—a spatter of white snow;
sunlight dimly rays the north window;
ice spreads its stiff crust over my iron inkstone.
Heedless of Heaven, heedless of men,
all I do is peck and polish away at my writings,
but words differ from east to west
and tastes of today belie those of the past.

1. "Encountering Sorrow," a long rhapsodic poem by the Chinese poet Ch'ü Yüan of the third cen. B.C.

My sentences are as ineffectual as the otter's sacrifice,[2]
my poems as pointless as a winter fan.
My one room opens to the north;
wind from the door crack pricks my face.
My mother lives here too—
fifty years old and never worn silk—
bustling bustling beside the blue lamp,
stitching clothes, eyes fixed on thread and needle.
I have no two acres of land—
couldn't retire to a life of farming.
I have no talent for saving the world—
could never put on official's cap.
"Poor means stupid!" people say—
down and out, I wince at their nasty saw.

2. According to ancient Chinese belief, the otter is performing a "sacrifice" when he leaves part of his prey uneaten.

TSUCHIYA KYŪTAI (1887–1958)

Atomic Bomb

A strange light, one thread falling from the blue—
suddenly the earth rocked, the sun in the sky went dark;
in the space of an instant, hills and valleys transformed,
a city, its towers and porches turned to dust and ash.
On that day three hundred thousand died,
the living covered with wounds, lamenting, groaning.
In the chaos, impossible to tell who died, who survived:
the wife searches for her husband, the child its parents.
Hell's moans and screams moving heaven and earth,
blood flowing in the streets, bodies strewn at every angle;
those who suffered, gave up their lives, no soldiers of war;
the victims of this horror were all innocent civilians.
Hiroshima struck with a disaster never known before;
enemy forces attack again, Nagasaki this time.
Two cities laid waste, even chickens and dogs wiped out;
crumbled walls, fallen tiles, no human being in sight.
Such heartless cruelty must rouse the ire of Heaven,
a brutality surpassing the wolves and tigers of Ch'in! [1]
Have you not heard them,
    the sighs of the spirits that weep from night till dawn?
In the broken cities dark with rain, their blue flames flicker.

---

1. The Ch'in dynasty in China in the third century B.C., notorious for
the cruelty and violence of its rule.

Part 2

Works by
the Monk Ryōkan

Ryōkan (1758–1831) was born in Izumozaki in the province of Echigo, in present-day Niigata Prefecture, the eldest son of a *nanushi* or village headman. In childhood he went by the name Yamamoto Eizō. At the age of seventeen, without receiving permission from his parents, he abruptly entered a local temple of the Sōtō branch of the Zen sect and began religious training. Some accounts say he became a monk immediately, adopting the religious name Ryōkan, others that he did not take this step until four years later. Meanwhile, his younger brother Yoshiyuki replaced him as family heir. It is not certain what impelled him to enter clerical life, though probably he did not feel qualified by temperament to succeed his father as village headman. In 1779 the Zen master Kokusen, head of the Entsū-ji in Bitchū in present-day Okayama Prefecture, happened to pass through Echigo and stopped at the temple where Ryōkan was residing. Ryōkan immediately determined to become his disciple and followed him back to the Entsū-ji, spending the next ten years or so there in Zen study under Kokusen's guidance. Eventually he gained enlightenment and received *inka*, the sanction of his teacher to become a Zen master in his own right. He left the Entsū-ji and spent some five years wandering about the country, though exactly where he went or how he lived is not known. In 1795 he returned to his native region, where he remained until his death. He stayed at a variety of temples in the area, and around 1804 settled down in the famous Gogō-an or Five Measures of Rice Retreat, a little hut on the slope of Mount Kugami, living there for the following thirteen years. When age made it difficult for him to hike up and down the mountain, he moved to the grounds of a Shinto shrine at the foot of it, and later to a renovated storehouse at the home of a friend in the village of Shimazaki, where he died at the age of seventy-three.

Unlike most distinguished Japanese Buddhist priests, he never headed a temple of his own, but lived entirely by *takuhatsu* or begging expeditions to nearby villages, or stayed with various families in the neighborhood. Though he had at least one lay disciple, he left no Dharma heir or successor to his religious teachings. He is famous for his *kanshi*, of which over four hundred are extant, as well as for his *waka* or poems in Japanese and his highly distinctive calligraphy. His poetry in Chinese is profoundly influenced by that of the T'ang dynasty recluse Han-shan, the Master of Cold Mountain, though he comes across as a somewhat warmer and more approachable personality than his idol. His works consciously ignore many of the technical niceties of traditional Chinese verse, and can perhaps best be appreciated in the light of the following declaration:

> Who says my poems are poems?
> My poems are not poems at all!
> Only when you understand that my poems are not poems
> can we begin to talk about poetry.

Most of Ryōkan's poems in Chinese are untitled and few can be dated accurately. The works in my selection are grouped mainly by subject.

✍ In High Spirits

Robe too short, jacket too long,
in high spirits, full of fight—that's how I get by.
On the road little boys suddenly spy me,
clap hands, all together give out with a *temari* song.[1]

1. A *temari* is a cloth ball wound with colored thread and used for various children's games, to which songs are sung.

✍ *Temari*[1]

In my sleeve the colored ball worth a thousand in gold;
I dare say no one's as good at *temari* as me!
And if you ask what it's all about—
one–two–three–four–five–six–seven

1. The ball described in the preceding poem and the games, particularly counting games, played with it.

✍ Grass Fight[1]

Again with the boys I fought a hundred grasses,
fought going, fought coming—what a brave fight we had!
Sun setting, lonely now, everyone gone home—
one round bright moon, whiter than autumn.

1. The "grass fight" is mentioned as early as T'ang times in China as a pastime played by girls on the fifth day of the fifth month, a genteel competition of grasses or flowers which was imported to Japan and pursued under the name *kusa-awase*. Ryōkan's grass fight, however, is a much more strenuous affair in which the contestant selects tough weed stalks, loops them around the stalks of his opponent, and conducts a tug-of-war.

Green spring, start of the second month,
colors of things turning fresh and new.
At this time I take my begging bowl,
in high spirits tramp the streets of town.
Little boys suddenly spot me,
delightedly come crowding around,
descend on me at the temple gate,
dragging on my arms, making steps slow.
I set my bowl on top of a white stone,
hang my alms bag on a green tree limb;
here we fight a hundred grasses,
here we hit the *temari* ball—
I'll hit, you do the singing!
Now I'll sing, your turn to hit!
We hit it going, hit it coming,
never knowing how the hours fly.
Passers-by turn, look at me and laugh,
"What makes you act like this?"
I duck my head, don't answer them—
I could speak but what's the use?
You want to know what's in my heart?
From the beginning, just this! just this!

Breath of spring bit by bit milder;
rattling the rings on my staff, I head for the east town.
Green green, willows in the gardens;
bobbing bobbing, duckweed on the pond.
Alms bowl smelling sweet with rice from a thousand houses;
heart indifferent to ten-thousand-chariot glory.[1]
Following in tracks of old time Buddhas,
begging for food, I go my way.

1. The glory and wealth of a ruler with an army of ten thousand chariots, an old Chinese expression.

Time: first day of the eighth month; [1]
with begging bowl I enter the city streets.
A thousand gates unbolted in the dawn;
A thousand homes where cooking smoke slants up.
Last night's rain washed the road clean;
autumn wind shakes the metal rings of my staff.
Taking my time, I go begging for food—
how wide, how boundless this Dharma world!

[1] Under the lunar calendar New Year came in early February and autumn comprised the seventh, eighth, and ninth lunar months.

✍ Empty Begging Bowl

Blue sky, cold wild-geese crying;
empty hills, tree leaves whirling.
Sunset, road through a hazy village:
going home alone, carrying an empty bowl.

✍ *Visited by Thieves*

My zazen platform, my cushion—they made off with both!
Thieves break into my grass hut, but who dares stop them?
All night I sit alone by the dark window,
soft rain pattering on the bamboo grove.

Dark of winter, eleventh month,
rain and snow slushing down;
a thousand hills all one color,
ten thousand paths where almost no one goes.
Past wanderings all turned to dreams;
grass gate, its leaves latched tight;
through the night I burn chips of wood,
quietly reading poems by men of long ago.

Shouldering firewood I climb down the green peak,
green peak where trails are never level.
Sometimes I rest under a tall pine,
listen quietly to the voice of spring birds.

As a boy I left my father, ran off to other lands,
tried hard to become a tiger—didn't even make it to cat!
If you ask what kind of man I am now,
just the same old Eizō I've always been.[1]

1. Eizō was Ryōkan's name before he became a monk.

All my life too lazy to try to get ahead,
I leave everything to the truth of Heaven.
In my sack three measures of rice,
by the stove one bundle of sticks—
why ask who's got satori, who hasn't?
What would I know about that dust, fame and gain?
Rainy nights here in my thatched hut
I stick out my two legs any old way I please.

Rags and tatters, rags and tatters,
rags and tatters—that's my life.
Food—somehow I pick it up along the road;
my house—I let the weeds grow all around.
Watching the moon, I spend the whole night mumbling poems;
lost in blossoms, I never come home.
Since I left the temple that trained me,
this is the kind of lazy old horse I've become.

On peaks before, peaks behind, snow glinting white;
my grass gate tightly shut, west of the rocky stream.
Through the long night in the fire pit I burn sticks of wood,
pulling on my beard, remembering times when I was young.

✍ Long Winter Night

I remember when I was young,
reading alone in the empty hall,
again and again refilling the lamp with oil,
never minding then how long the winter night was.

Done with a long day's begging,
I head home, close the wicker door,
in the stove burn branches with the leaves still on them,
quietly reading Cold Mountain poems.
West wind blasts the night rain,
gust on gust drenching the thatch.
Now and then I stick my legs out, lie down—
what's there to think about, what's the worry?

✍ Dialogue in a Dream

Begging food, I went to the city,
on the road met a wise old man.
He asked me, "Master, what are you doing
living there among those white-clouded peaks?"
I asked him, "Sir, what are you doing
growing old in the middle of this red city dust?"
We were about to answer, but neither had spoken
when fifth-watch bells shattered my dream.

I have a walking stick—
don't know how many generations it's been handed down—
the bark peeled off long ago,
nothing left but a sturdy core.
In past years it tested the depth of a stream,
how many times clanged over steep rocky trails!
Now it leans against the east wall,
neglected, while the flowing years go by.

In a flash of lightning, sixty years;
world's glory and decay—clouds that come and go.
Deep night rains about to gouge out the foot of the cliff;
wick of the lamp glowing, guttering by the old window.

(In his later years the poet moved from his mountain hut, the Gogō-an, to the Otogo Shrine at the southern foot of Mount Kugami, living there for the following ten years.)

As a boy I studied literature,
>   but was too lazy to become a Confucian;
in my young days I worked at Zen,
>   but got no Dharma worth handing down.
Now I've built a grass hut,
>   act as custodian of a Shinto shrine,
half a shrine man,
>   half a monk.

(The "twelve divisions" are the twelve sections into which the Buddhist scriptures are divided. The poem is an attack on the kind of sectarianism common in Chinese and Japanese Buddhism that seeks to exalt the verity and worth of one sutra over that of all the others.)

Buddha preached the twelve divisions,
each division full of purest truth.
East wind—rain comes in the night,
making all the forests fresh and new.
No sutra that does not save the living,
no branch in the forest not visited by spring.
Learn to understand the meaning in them,
don't try to decide which is "valid," which is not!

✍ To Inscribe on a Picture of a Skull I Painted

All things born of causes end when causes run out;
but causes, what are they born of?
That very first cause—where did it come from?
At this point words fail me, workings of my mind go dead.
I took these words to the old woman in the house to the east;
the old woman in the house to the east was not pleased.
I questioned the old man in the house to the west;
the old man in the house to the west puckered his brow
      and walked away.
I tried writing the question on a biscuit, fed it to the dogs,
but even the dogs refused to bite.
Concluding that these must be unlucky words, a mere jumble
      of a query,
I rolled life and death into a pill, kneading them together,
and gave it to the skull in the meadowside.
Suddenly the skull came leaping up,
began to sing and dance for me,
a long song, ballad of the Three Ages,
a wonderful dance, postures of the Three Worlds.[1]
Three worlds, three ages, three times danced over—
"the moon sets on Ch'ang-an and its midnight bells." [2]

1. The three ages of past, present, and future; the three worlds of desire, form, and formlessness.

2. The last line is taken verbatim from a poem entitled "For the Monk San-tsang on His Return to the Western Regions" by the 9th-century Chinese poet Li Tung, translated in my *Chinese Lyricism* (New York: Columbia University Press, 1971), p. 120.

✍ Drinking Wine with Yoshiyuki and Being Very Happy

(Yoshiyuki was Ryōkan's brother, four years his junior.)

Older and younger brother meet—
both with white eyebrows drooping down.
And what delight in this time of peace,
day after day getting drunk as fools!

⚰ When News of Saichi's Death Arrived

(Miwa Saichi was a *koji* or layman who studied Zen with Ryōkan until his death in the fifth month of 1807. To Ryōkan, who apparently had few other Zen students, his death was a great blow, and he referred to it often in his poems.)

Ah—my *koji!*
studied Zen with me twenty years.
You were the one who understood—
things I couldn't pass on to other men.

I Dreamt of Saichi and Woke with a Feeling of Uneasiness

After twenty some years, one meeting with you,
gentle breeze, hazy moon, east of the country bridge;
we walked on and on, hand in hand, talking,
till we reached the Hachiman Shrine in your village of Yoita.

My one aim, to be a wandering monk,
how could I have lingered any longer?
Lugging a water jug, I took leave of my old teacher,
in high spirits set off for other parts,
mornings climbing to the top of the lone peak,
evenings crossing the dark sea's flow.
And while one word fails to match the Truth,
I vow all my life never to rest!

I remember when I was at Entsū-ji,
always sorry my way was such a solitary one.
Hauling firewood, I thought of Mr. P'ang;
treadling the pounder, I recalled old Lu.[1]
At *nisshitsu* I never dared to be last,
at morning *sanzen* always got there first.[2]
Since I left my place at the temple,
thirty long years have passed.
Mountains and seas lie between me and that land,
no one to bring me any news.
I think of the debt I owe my teacher, end in tears—
let them flow, flow to the river.

1. Mr. P'ang is the layman or *koji* P'ang, a devout Zen believer of T'ang times whose sayings have been preserved. Old Lu is Hui-neng, the famous Sixth Patriarch of Chinese Zen in the eighth century, who for a time worked at the temple pounding rice in a treadle-operated mortar.

2. *Nisshitsu* refers to the private interview between the Zen master and the student; *sanzen* here probably indicates the morning meditation period or some other morning ceremony.

Bothered by Something

I shaved my head, became a monk,
plowed through the weeds, spent years looking for the Way.
Yet now wherever I go they hand me paper and brush,
and all they say is "Write us a *waka!*" "Write us a Chinese
    poem!"

✍ Seventh Month, Sixteenth Day

Where to escape this steamy heat?
I like best the Izuruta Shrine.[1]
Miiin-miiin, the shrill of locusts fills my ears;
cool cool breezes come out of the wood.

1. A little local shrine at the village of Shimazaki, where the poet lived
shortly before his death.

Part 3

WORKS BY RAI SAN'YŌ

Rai San'yō (1781–1832) was the only surviving son of a Confucian scholar named Rai Shunsui of the fief of Aki in present-day Hiroshima Prefecture. His mother Baishi was the daughter of a Confucian scholar and physician of Osaka, where San'yō's father ran a small private school and where San'yō was born. Shortly after, his father was invited to become an official Confucian scholar of his native fief, and he and his family returned to Takehara in Aki. San'yō began his studies under his uncle Rai Kyōhei. He was extremely bright, diligent in his work and especially fond of history, but physically rather weak and so moody and temperamental that his parents could barely manage him. At the age of seventeen he went to Edo with his uncle and became a student in the Shōheikō, the school for Confucian studies operated by the shogunate. But for reasons no biographer has so far been able to ascertain for certain—though there are rumors of a sexual indiscretion—he left the school after a year and returned home.

His parents, hoping that marriage would settle him down, arranged for him to take as a bride the fourteen-year-old daughter of a local physician. The marriage failed to have the desired effect, however, and the bride, reduced to a state of hysteria, returned to her own home. She was already pregnant and bore a son, named Mototada or Itsuan, who was adopted and raised by San'yō's father. Meanwhile, San'yō ran away from Aki, a grave offense, since official permission was required for all journeys outside one's own fief. He was eventually located in Kyoto and brought home, where, as a result of his parents' pleas, he was pardoned from more severe punishment on grounds of insanity and placed under house arrest. He was disinherited and a cousin adopted as heir in his place.

San'yō spent his term in confinement studying and writing, beginning the work that in time was to make him famous, the *Nihon gaishi* or *Unofficial History of Japan*, a lengthy history in Chinese dealing with the various military families that had wielded power in the period from the late years of the Heian to the beginning of the Tokugawa era.

After three years of confinement, he was permitted to move about freely and was sent to study with a friend of his father's, Kan Sazan, a scholar and poet of the neighboring province of Bingo. In 1811, after a year or so of study under Kan Sazan, he went to Kyoto, where he opened a private school. Though making frequent trips home to Aki and elsewhere, he resided in Kyoto for the remainder of his life. As his fame as a historian, *kanshi* poet, amateur painter, and man of taste spread, the number of his students and patrons increased, and he was able to live fairly comfortably.

In 1815 he married Hikita Rie, who bore him three sons, Tatsuzō (died in childhood), Matajirō or Shihō, and Mikisaburō or Ōgai, and a daughter. His father died in 1816, but his mother lived until 1843 and often journeyed to Kyoto to visit her son. San'yō, no doubt troubled by guilt over the grief he had caused his parents in his youth, treated his mother with great affection and respect and wrote of her often in his poems. In 1827 he presented a copy of his *Nihon gaishi* to the eminent statesman Matsudaira Sadanobu, who was by this time living in retirement and had requested to see the work. Matsudaira praised it highly and eventually, some ten years after San'yō's death, it was printed. It ran through numerous editions and enjoyed enormous popularity in the closing years of the Tokugawa era. Though of dubious value as history, the work was highly admired for its elegant Chinese prose style and its expressions of

support for the imperial house. It continued to be read enthusiastically in the Meiji period, as attested by the words of the
famous critic Okakura Tenshin (1862–1913), who described it as
"that epic narrative of the country from whose poetic pages the
youth of Japan still learn the intensity of the raging fever that
moved their grandfathers to revolution." [1] Rai San'yō's poems
and other prose pieces in Chinese were also widely distributed
and admired. He continued active at his historical and literary
endeavors until his death in 1832 at the age of fifty-one.

In recent years in Japan there has been a sharp reaction
against the kind of ebullient adulation evident in Okakura's appraisal, and an almost perverse determination to prove that
San'yō's reputation is undeserved. There is no doubt that he
was an indifferent historian, and his celebrated political views
were no more original or daring than those of countless of his
contemporaries. His forte was not intellectual analysis, and his
historical writings bear no comparison with those of more objec-
tive and penetrating scholars such as Arai Hakuseki. His aim in
his poems and meditations on history was rather to recreate and
dramatize the events of the past, a task at which he was, in literary terms, eminently successful, while his writings on the contemporary scene excel in breadth of subject and sympathy of
treatment. Like his idol Sugawara no Michizane centuries earlier, he had made himself the master of his medium, and for that
reason was able to employ it with a facility and creativeness all
but unmatched in the Edo period. When the dust of controversy
has settled and he has ceased to be castigated for his shortcom-
ings as a thinker and historian, his stature as a writer of poetry
and prose in Chinese will, I believe, remain unshaken.

1. Okakura, Kakuzo, *The Ideals of the East* (New York: E. P. Dutton &
Co., 1904; reprinted by Charles E. Tuttle: Rutland, Vermont &
Tokyo, Japan, 1970), p. 210; the book was written in English.

✍ Visiting my father, I wrote this to match the rhymes of my elders Kan and Koga.

(Fourth month, ninth day, 1814, on a visit to his home in Hiroshima. The poem employs the same rhymes as the poems composed on the occasion by the Confucian scholar Koga Seiri (1750–1817) and by his teacher Kan Sazan.)

Chill on the grain, we can't put up our padded quilts,
though beyond the willows now and then I hear an oriole.
A wandering son, worried at heart by the passing days,
my old father, short hair showing the touch of autumn.[1]
New-bought books piled in heaps, propping up the shelf;
old flowering trees I remember, now taller than the house.
My mother—many thanks—hasn't forgotten my favorite dish,
with her own hand cooks bamboo shoots from the garden—the
      "cat's head" kind.

1. The poet worries about his father's advanced age, especially as he notices how gray his father's hair is getting.

✍ Setting out from Hiroshima,
Saying Goodby to My Father

(Ninth month, eleventh day, 1814, starting off for Kyoto after a visit with his father Shunsui and other family members in Hiroshima; Shunsui died two years later.)

Hurrying, hurrying, we've downed our cups of wine;
slowly, reluctantly, I go out the neighborhood gate,
turning my head, asking my cousins
to be good enough to look after my parents for me.
The boat moves forward, islands shift, city receding in the
      distance;
far off I see my well-wishers turn back from the shore.
One tree like a carriage top looms in the gathering dusk:
I can still make out the camphor that grows by my father's gate.

✍ Inscribed on Landscapes I Painted Myself

(The first of six poems with this title; 1817.)

Tung, Chü, Ni, Huang—I've never laid eyes on them; [1]
I only know rocks pile up into peaks.
Sketches conceived in my head, done in my own style—
don't tell me in this world there are no such mountains!

---

1. The famous Chinese landscape painters Tung Yüan and Chü-jan of the Sung, and Ni Tsan and Huang Kung-wang of the Yuan.

✍ Written on Visiting the Shrine of the Minister of the Right Sugawara no Michizane at the Dazaifu

(1818. Sugawara no Michizane (845–903), a Confucian scholar and poet, rose to high office at court but in 901 was slandered by rivals of the Fujiwara clan and forced into exile at the Dazaifu, a government office near Hakata in northern Kyushu. After his death he was deified as the god Temmangū Tenjin, patron of learning, and shrines were set up to him throughout the country. The opening lines are from a famous poem in Chinese by him written in exile and entitled "On Not Going Out the Gate" [see my *Japanese Literature in Chinese*, Vol. 1 (New York: Columbia University Press, 1975, p. 111.)])

"Government office tower—I can just see the tint of its tiles;
Kannon Temple—I can only hear the sound of its bell."
These lines of his I used to recite as a boy;
today for the first time I've come to the spot.
I imagine the stately building with its tiers of flowered tiles,
the brave boom of the great patterned bell from the Buddhist
    temple.
Though he held an empty title, in fact he was an outcast,
brooding on faults, keeping his brushwood gate closed.[1]
Rare for a Confucian scholar to don the robes of high office;
for so long, family alone counted in promotion.
Perceiving the grave ills of the state, he administered
    good medicine,

1. Michizane was given a nominal official title in the Dazaifu, though in fact he was a virtual prisoner in his house. The lines that follow refer to Michizane's efforts to curb the power of the Fujiwara family and the eventual decline of the court and rise of the military class.

with fierce will wielded sharp tools to cut out the root of evil.
Offering his wisdom, what leisure had he to worry what others
said?
Struggling fiercely, he broke the wings that might have carried
him over the clouds.
Men play the devil, the demon?—why let that trouble you?
The lone crane shuns and is shunned by flocks of common fowl.
The distress of the state was fated—what did it have to do
with you?
Already the warrior's mirrored belt, his vermilion bow.
Like drifting clouds, how often has the way of the world
changed?
Your merit alone still handed down ages without end.
The crossbeams of your shrine soar loftier, higher;
numberless worshipers bring offerings to you today.
I search for the government office tower, find only broken
basestones;
of the temple nothing remains but a few sagging shacks.
Strolling the fields, I pick up bits of shattered tile,
perhaps the very ones whose tints you saw.

✍ Dutch Ship

(Written in the summer of 1818 on a visit to Nagasaki.)

In Nagasaki Bay, southwest where sky and water meet,
suddenly at heaven's edge a tiny dot appears.
The cannon of the lookout tower gives one roar
and in twenty-five watch stations bows are bared.
Through the streets on four sides the cry breaks forth:
"The redhaired Westerners are coming!"
Launches set out to meet them, we hear the drum echo,
in the distance signal flags are raised to stay alarm.
The ship enters the harbor like a ponderous turtle,
so huge that in the shallows it seems certain to ground.
Our little launches, so many strings of pearls,
tow it forward amid a clamorous din.
The barbarian hull rises a hundred feet from the surface,
sea winds sighing, flapping its pennants of felt.
Three sails stretched among ten thousand lines,
fixed to engines moving up and down like wellsweeps.
Blackskinned slaves nimble as monkeys
scale the masts, haul the lines, keeping them from tangling.[1]
The anchor drops with shouts from the crew,
giant cannon bellow forth roar after roar.
Barbarian hearts are hard to fathom; the Throne ponders,
aware that defenses are far from complete.
Ah, the wretches, why do they come to vex our eyes,
pursuing ten thousand miles their greed for gain,

1. Javanese servants of the Dutch.

their ships pitiful leaves upon the monstrous waves,
drawn like giant ants to rancid meat?
Do we not bear ox-knives to kill a mere chicken,
trade our most precious jewels for thorns? [2]

2. I.e., are not all the alarms and defense measures of the government
unnecessary, and are we not losing by trading with the foreigners?
Confucian-oriented scholars like Rai San'yō could see nothing good in
commerce.

✍ Songs of Satsuma

(1818; second of ten poems with this title. The lord of Satsuma in Kyushu, who took part in Hideyoshi's invasion of Korea at the end of the sixteenth century, brought back with him as prisoners some eighty Korean potters and established a pottery industry in his domain which in time produced the famous Satsuma ware. Kōrai is another name for Korea.)

On the road I meet descendants of the Korean prisoners,
men who work as potters, live in a village apart.
How wonderful—that from this clay of Japan
they can fashion Kōrai bowls in the shapes of the past!

✍ Coming Home

(Third month, eleventh day, 1819; returning to his home at Nijō Taka-kura in Kyoto after over a year of travel in western Japan.)

To the end of the alley sloshing through new mud,
dawn rain coming down now in thin threads;
the nearer home, the more nervous I feel,
wondering if I'll recognize the old house.
My wife recalls the sound of my step,
so filled with joy she seems to be grieving.
Two years, my first time home,
face black with dust of the road.
She heats water to wash my feet,
but the wood is damp and slow to burn.
Slow to burn—what does that matter!
Happiness enough in this meeting alone.

✍ Mount Yoshino

(Three poems written on a visit to Mount Yoshino in Yamato made by
the poet and his mother in the fourth month of 1819. The mountain is
famous for its cherries, though by the time the poet arrived they had
for the most part finished blooming.)

1

I attend her palanquin a hundred miles, crossing rugged slopes;
blossoms shed, the southern mountain in a thousand new shades
    of green.
Bamboo shoots, ferns to go with the wine in an evening inn:
in my mother's kindly face, the full bloom of spring.

2

Ten thousand heaps of fragrant snow fallen in the dust—
I'm sorry we ever made this trip to Yoshino.
But by streamside trails, where cold lingers, a token of good
    will—
a few cherries have held back their blossoms, opening after
    the others!

3

On flowered paths, squeaks of flying squirrels—I can't spot
    them anywhere;
temples, their towers and porches noisy with merrymakers.
Cryptomeria and cedar reach to the sky, blackening the spring
    sun;
an overgrown gravemound—who mourns for Go-Daigo? [1]

1. Emperor Go-Daigo, who attempted to assert the power of the
throne, was forced by military opponents to flee from Kyoto and take
refuge on Mount Yoshino, where he died in 1339. He was one of the
figures most admired by the poet, who was undoubtedly disappointed
that so few visitors to the mountain showed respect for the emperor's
grave.

Shortly after I married, I had to go into mourning for my father.[1] *Now I have a son. I wrote these to express my joy.*

(The first three of six poems written on the birth of his son Tatsuzō on the seventh day of the tenth month, 1820.)

1

No fields, no house, one poor scholar,
but I have a child, and to my delight it's a boy!
A few paintings, a pair of old inkstones:
your father offers them to you—but will you accept them?

2

So stupid of me to hope you'll take to books;
a scholar all my life, I want to raise you the same way.
Baby squalls that to other ears are nothing but noise—
sooner or later they'll give way to the student's drone.

3

Fist like the mountain fern half unfurled,
skin like the pomegranate when the blossom has just dropped;
all you do is howl, searching for your mother's breast;
beautiful baby eyes that have not learned to tell their father.

1. Almost no Japanese in Tokugawa times observed the traditional Confucian 25-month mourning period for parents. San'yō, however, probably out of feelings of guilt, did so, though in a deliberately unostentatious manner. The mourning involved abstinence from meat, wine, and sexual relations, which is why he mentions it here.

✍ Landscape Vignettes

(Second and third of five poems with this title written in 1821.)

1

I put away my book, chin in hand, alone,
watching homing birds in the woods over there,
mumbling over a poem, can't decide on the right word,
as evening shades gather by the corner of the eaves.

2

Out the gate I meet a friend
coming to visit me with a poem in his sleeve.
Plenty of time to look at your poem later—
first let's go together to see the plums in bloom.

🖋 The Cat in Cold Weather

(One of four "Songs of the Cold" written in 1821 and inspired in part
by a similar series by the Ch'ing poet Chiang Shih-ch'üan, 1725–1785.)

Witless and dull, I curl up in the hut I love,
laughing that my laziness is so much like yours.
A cramped room all smokey—what rat would live here?
My poor kitchen grown cold—you'll find no fish there!
Through the long night on the quilt corner you share my sleep,
in midday warmth sit with me by the brazier's side.
And now you're off yowling for your lady love—
silhouetting the plum by the eaves next door, a moon just
     coming up.

✍ New House

(In the eleventh month of 1822, San'yō moved to a new house on the west bank of the Kamo River just north of present-day Marutamachi which he called Suiseisō or Villa West of the River. The poem was written on New Year's day, which, according to traditional reckoning in China and Japan, marked the beginning of spring.)

In a new house greeting the first of the year,
opening doors on bright clear weather:
below the stairs, shallow water flows,
rippling already with the sound of spring.
Bending by the current, I wash my inkstone,
purple of the stone reflecting green of hills.
In such an out-of-the-way spot, few visitors—
I'm pleased to be spared all that greeting and goodbying.
A place to live this peaceful—
it fits exactly with what I've always wanted;
only I regret that business of my mother,
not arranging to have her come live with me.
How can I share this wine with her,
see her gentle face smiling as she lifts the cup?
I grind some ink, write a letter home
in a drunken hand that keeps straying out of line.

✍ Written on New Year's Eve

(On the last night of 1824. Anyone who has seen the furious activity that goes on in a traditional Japanese household at such a time will immediately recognize the scene.)

My wife rushing around, hair like a tangle of hemp,
maid preparing New Year's dishes, groom sweeping the house—
the old man, the only one with nothing to do,
goes out to stroll the neighboring lanes, looking for
      blossoming plum.

🖎 I accompanied my uncle Shumpō on an outing to Lake Biwa and wrote this to commemorate the occasion.

(Third month, 1825; Hirai Kisō lived at Ōsaka Barrier on the road between Kyoto and Lake Biwa.)

My father and my uncle
once accompanied my grandfather—
so often I've heard of that youthful expedition,
how they bought wine, drank in a tower by the lake;
their old friend Hirai Kisō
served as host along the eastern road.
Now my father, my grandfather, and my father's friend
all are logged in ledgers of the dead;
only my uncle is still with me
as we set out to retrace that former outing.
I live now by the Kyoto bridge,
take his hand carefully, help him along.
At the stone landing we rent a little boat,
riding together, listening to the gentle oars.
He points out spots of that earlier trip,
some forty-five years ago:
"Weather was clear, the lake calm,
not like the rain we've run into today.
From the lake we could see the mountains
ranged peak by peak, all plainly in view!"
The dead will never see them again,
and the living—how often will we be together?
Uncle and nephew have a chance to tip the cup;

where shall we buy our presents for those at home?
I'm learning to wash away my cares with wine,
dancing a crazy dance to delight the elders.
Still I can't help worrying about my boy,
troubled in mind by the sickness that racks him.[1]
But why speak of wife and family—
my uncle is the guest of honor today.
I've written this poem to mark the occasion,
a footnote to add to the family records.

1. The poet's five-year-old son Tatsuzō, who had been stricken with smallpox.

✍ Grieving for Tatsuzō: Today Spring Ended

(Third month, twenty-ninth day, 1825; the poet's son Tatsuzō died the previous day of smallpox.)

Goodby to spring, goodby to my son,
two bitter sorrows today.
Spring leaves us to come another day,
but my dead boy I'll never see again.
Flowers of deception for a moment delight the eye—
how craftily the Creator toys with men!
Next year in eastern fields when I search the paths of spring,
who will lug the wine gourd, tag after the old man?

✒ Mourning for My Younger Sister

(On the death of his sister Miho, his only sibling, who died on the ninth day of the seventh month of 1826.)

Sudden bad news—reading, I couldn't believe it—
only last fall you wrote your brother that letter!
I feel my face and form grow twice as old and withered—
on this old tree of ours, only one branch left.

✍ Random Thoughts on the Writing of History

(The second and eighth of ten poems with this title written in 1827, when the poet had just finished the final draft of his renowned work of history, the *Nihon gaishi*.)

1

I chastise the bones of an old villain of a thousand years ago,
comfort a soul that suffered injustice, gone to lands of the dead.
Who says the writing brush has no power?
On paper—that's where right in the end will be decided!

2

Twenty-some years and I've finished my book;
before it I pour a libation of wine, tug at my beard.
All those old heroes here in the book—
because of *me* their true stories can now be told!

✒ Twenty-seven Quatrains Discussing Poetry

(The next to the last in the series. Though listed under the date 1827, the poems were probably composed over a considerable period of time. Most deal with Japanese *kanshi* poets, from Sugawara no Michizane to San'yō's contemporaries, but this one expresses the view on how to write *kanshi* which prevailed in San'yō's time.)

In form most people look to Sung and Yuan models;
for mood, they strive to capture Middle or Late T'ang flavors.
Bits of beauty, scattered scents, shaped to the taste
     of the time—
why must you work so hard to copy Han and Su? [1]

1. Han Yü and Su Tung-p'o were two of the Chinese poets whom San'yō most admired and took as his models, the others being Tu Fu and Lu Yu. San'yō asks himself why he bothers to try to write good poetry in their style rather than following along with the shallow tastes of the time.

🖋 *I heard of Master Kan's illness but couldn't get there in time; I composed these to voice my grief.*

(One of four poems on the death of the poet's teacher Kan Sazan in the eighth month of 1827. The poet set out from Kyoto but reached Kannabe in Bingo only after his teacher's death.)

I heard of the illness, raced a thousand miles,
along the road got notice of his death.
I couldn't be there to help haul the coffin,
hate myself for having started out so late!
The old house, willows where they always were;
empty room, lamp glowing bright—
what pain to hear of his dying words
entrusting me to put his papers in order.

✍ The Mongols Are Coming!

(One of the *Nihon gafu* or "Ballads of Japan," a series of sixty-six poems on famous events in Japanese history cast in *yüeh-fu* or ballad form, which uses lines of varying lengths. The series, modeled on similar works by the Ming poet Li Tung-yang and completed in 1828, enjoyed wide popularity. The following work deals with the attempted Mongol invasions of the thirteenth century. Ardently patriotic poems such as this helped to inspire the Japanese in later years when they faced the Western powers clamoring for the opening of the country.)

From the sea of Tsukushi a great wind blows, blackening the
      sky:
spread over the sea, who are these pirates who come?
The Mongols are coming,
coming from the north!
Bit by bit they hope to eat their way east and west,
terrorizing the old widow of the house of Chao; [1]
now they prepare to advance on the islands of Japan.
Tarō of Sagami has courage big as a barrel; [2]
defending the coast, each general and soldier exerts all the
                strength he has.
The Mongols are coming,
but we're not afraid!
We only fear orders from Kamakura, stern as mountains,
that command us to destroy the invader, permit no second
      thought.

1. Empress Dowager Yang, mother of the child emperor of the Sung dynasty, which the Mongols overthrew in 1279.

2. The Kamakura Regent Hōjō Tokimune, who defied the Mongols and took measures to repulse them.

We'll unstep our masts,
board the invaders' vessels,
seize their vile leaders—
hear our army shout! [3]
Hateful—these eastern winds that raced with the great waves,
kept us from bathing Japanese swords in their beastly blood! [4]

3. This refers to an actual incident in which one of the Japanese military leaders went out in a small boat to meet the Mongol fleet, used his mast to board the enemy vessel, and seized its commander.

4. The Mongol fleets were twice destroyed by typhoons that struck as they were attempting to invade Kyushu.

✍ Reading Books

(The third and sixth of eight poems with this title written in 1828.)

1

This morning, splendid breeze and sunlight,
north window where the new rain passed;
visitors sent off, I open my book;
then my wife comes with her story:
"No money coming in—all these relatives—
eight mouths—how can we get along alone?
No one important ever comes to call—
poverty and cold—that's all we'll ever know!
If only you'd be a little less sharp—
try being pleasant to others for a change—"
My illness, who can cure it?
The bones I have are the ones Heaven gave me.
If I'd stayed in my father's fief
I'd never have forgone official service.
But if I went back to that petty routine,
wouldn't I be false to my father's hopes?
Go away—don't bother me!
I'm trying to converse with the men of old.[1]

---

1. Despite the gruff tone, San'yō was apparently very devoted to his wife, and in fact was known in current parlance as a *rakuda* or "camel," a man who, contrary to custom, takes his wife along with him on outings and social visits.

2

Eastern hills—dense and lush,
turning purple in the evening sun.
Kamo River ripples have all subsided,
only here and there the glint of a white gem.
Our family ducks know the day is ended;
they quack to each other, time to go home!
I too put away my books,
call to my wife to get out the cask of wine.
Fresh fish from the river, just right for grilling;
bamboo shoots—we dig them ourselves.
I'm going to sit by the eastern eaves,
share a drink with the hills over there.

✒ Isuzu River

(Third month, 1829, on a visit to the Grand Shrine at Ise which the poet made with his mother. The Isuzu River is where worshipers purify themselves before entering the shrine, dedicated to the Sun Goddess, the ancestress of the imperial family.)

Level ground breathing clouds of vapor;
towering to the sky, trees heaping up deep shade:
where the Goddess has dwelled for ten thousand years,
where the hearts of the numberless multitudes are drawn.
These waters flowing on, now as in the past—
what man can tell if they be shallow or deep?
Wily heroes who plot against her descendants
can never escape the Sun that looks down.

✍ Escorting My Mother Home:
a Short Song for the Road

(In the spring of 1829 the poet's mother came to visit him in Kyoto. In the fall of the same year he escorted her part of the way back home to Hiroshima.)

East winds to greet my mother when she came;
north winds see her on her way back home.
She arrived when roads were fragrant with blossoms,
now suddenly this cold of frost and snow!
At cock crow already I'm tying my footgear,
waiting by her palanquin, legs a bit unsteady.
Never mind if the son's legs are tired,
just worry whether her palanquin's fit for riding.
I pour her a cup of wine, a drink for myself too,
first sunlight flooding the inn, frost already dried.
Fifty-year-old son, seventy-year-old mother—
not often you find a pair lucky as we!
Off to the south, in from the north, streams of people—
who among them happy as this mother and son?

𝄢 Farewell Talk with Saikō by a Rainy Window

(The intercalary third month of 1830. Saikō is Ema Saikō (1787–1861), daughter of the physician and scholar of Dutch learning Ema Ransai of Mino. She studied *kanshi* writing under San'yō; see p. 58. San'yō fell in love with her in his early thirties and asked his friend Yanagawa Seigan to arrange a marriage. Saikō's father refused to consent, and though he later relented, by that time San'yō had given up hope and in 1815 took Hikita Rie as his second wife. The poem suggests that San'yō was still in love with her fifteen years later.)

A parting meal, low lamp—stay and enjoy it a bit longer;
new mud on the road home—better wait till it dries.
On peaks across the river, clouds only now dispersing;
strings and songs in the house next door just beginning to fade
      in the night.
Intercalary month this spring—my guest lingers on,
though last night's rain heartlessly scattered the cherry flowers.
From here you go to Mino—not a long way away,
though, growing old, I know how hard it is to meet now and
      then.

✍ Hearing of the earthquake in Kyoto, I wrote this to express my anxiety.

(Seventh month, 1830; written when on a visit to Hiroshima.)

By post, news from the capital,
an occurrence like nothing in the past:
this month, the second day,
earthquakes from dusk to dawn.
Later reports say that for seven days and nights
tremors went on till the earth seemed about to split.
People weeping, screaming, crying to Heaven—
of ten houses, eight or nine destroyed,
whole families spreading mats in the street
as roof tiles rained down to left and right.
Of my family not a word—
I gaze east, scratching my head,
imagining my house on the Kamo bank,
little ones clinging to my frail wife,
pulling each other along, fleeing to river sands,
though fearful at leaving the house unguarded.
Stone embankments must have crumbled completely,
nothing left but bare willow roots.
Currents deep, the shoals far off,
they don't know which way to run,
the older boy big enough to wade,
the little one on his nurse's back.
Nest overturned, though all escape alive,
the mother must be sick with care,
bearing all alone the worries of the family—

how can I ever face you again?
I wrote a letter, sent it speeding back,
wait ten days and more, still no answer.
Not even knowing if you're alive or dead,
where in this chaos can I turn for news?
When such terrors strike the multitudes,
how can one ask of him or her?
Rumors come of His Majesty,
aloof from affairs of state,
impassive, entrusting all to others—
is this why anger is visited on us?
Who am I to dare voice concern?
All of us gaze upward with reverent salute.
Osaka must have felt the tremors;
Edo—was it stricken too?
The price of rice bound to soar,
millions of mouths gape in hunger.
I recall tales of Temmei disasters,
when all three cities were afflicted,
how Mount Asama shook and crumbled
and the starving rose up to trample each other.[1]
The fate of Heaven moves by cycles;
on earth, who should bear the blame?
I watch the clouds hurrying north,
dragons of the sea rain howl.
Needless, perhaps, but my heart is troubled
as I beat out the measures of this long song.

1. The famines of the Temmei era, which lasted from 1782–87 and wiped out close to a million persons, were caused by floods and unseasonable weather and afflicted the entire country. The eruption of Mt. Asama in Shinshū in 1783 added to the distress.

✍ Returning Home

(Eighth month, sixth day, 1830.)

After the earthquake, returning to the capital,
changing at Fushimi landing,
tying up the boat, climbing Yodo Bridge,
renting a palanquin, I set out by Toba Road.
I can see the cracks left in the roadway
as we wind along by the light of torches.
I peer around in the glow they cast:
houses toppled over, not yet repaired,
fallen tiles piled in mounds,
leaning walls barely propped up with beams;
but the highway pretty much as it's always been;
I reach home as the fourth drum sounds.[1]
House little as ever, but not badly damaged,
buildings look to be the same as before.
The people inside, wary of intruders—
I hear them talking but they're afraid to open the door.
My wife, with face drawn and weary,
calls the boys to get up and greet their father.
Putting up with sickness, I've hurried a thousand miles,
wanting to see you as soon as I could.[2]
I ask how it was when the earthquake struck;
trying to answer, the terror shows in your faces.

1. Around ten in the evening.

2. The poet was not well at the time and suffered particularly from diarrhea during his trip to Hiroshima.

155

The maid and groom came forward to put in their word,
lamp wick raised, all talking at once.
Walls and roof more or less patched up,
rice and firewood are still an endless worry.
Never mind, just warm some wine—
everyone safe—that's the real joy!

✍ The Day After Saying Goodby to Mototada

(Fourth month, sixteenth day, 1831. Mototada, better known by his literary name Itsuan, was the poet's eldest son, on his way to Edo after journeying from Aki and spending one evening with his father in Kyoto. San'yō saw him off as far as Seta Bridge at the south end of Lake Biwa.)

Yesterday by the lake bridge, parting hands, returning;
I count on my fingers, wondering what relay stop you've
     reached by now.
With this spell of good weather, you can push on without delay;
raise the shade of your palanquin—you may see the crest of
    Fuji!

*⚞ I accompanied my mother on a visit to the
Itsukushima Shrine. She told me that when
I was two years old, she and my father took
me to visit my grandfather, and afterward
paid a visit to the shrine.*

(Tenth month, eighteenth day, 1831, the second of two poems.)

My father and mother held me in their arms, climbing out
    of the boat,
a baby swaddled, strapped on the back as they bowed before
    the shrine.
white haired mother and son come once more to pray—
some vanish, some survive—fifty long long years.

✍ New Year's Day

(1832. The poet's eldest son was in Edo at the residence of the Asano family, the lords of Aki, at Sakurada; his mother was ill in Hiroshima.)

In Sakurada quarters, dawn breaking, scrambling into his
      clothes;
my mother's room, past noon, her New Year's cup untasted:
welcoming spring this year, my heart is tugged many ways—
west with thoughts of my mother, east with thoughts of my son.

✍ *Delighted that Jippo has come to see me in my illness, I wrote this.*

(Ninth month, ninth day, 1832. Kōda Jippo was a physician who evidently journeyed from the eastern side of Lake Biwa to visit the poet.)

I'm ashamed, with this set of discordant bones,
to be lingering still between heaven and earth.
Who told you of my sudden turn for the worse,
troubled you to come journeying across lake and hill?
You rowed the waves from Yabase landing,
in wind palanquined over Ōsaka barrier.[1]
An old man with nothing but tears
greets you, but can't seem to manage a smile.

1. Yabase is on the east side of Lake Biwa; Ōsaka Barrier is on the road between Ōtsu, on the west side of the lake, and Kyoto; see p. 139.

✍ A Parting Talk with Seigan

(On the seventeenth day of the ninth month of 1832 Yanagawa Seigan, about to leave for Edo, called on Rai San'yō to inquire of his health. San'yō knew it was the last time he would see his friend; he died six days later.)

Lamp by the yellow chrysanthemums,
    close onto midnight;
tomorrow morning you set off
    to tread the Shinshū clouds.
Our one pot of wine gone,
    but stay a little longer—
in this sickness near to death,
    must I say goodby to you?

✍ The Biography of Yuri

Higashiyama is one of the loveliest spots in Kyoto. Each year when the cherries bloom, rare silks and gauzes mill and throng about; strings and songs, babble and hubbub, dropped earrings and forgotten hairpins fill the lanes; and the sea of all this caroling and piping is the place called Makuzugahara. Whenever I read the poem on Makuzugahara and its air of desolation by the priest Jien (1155–1225), I never fail to marvel at how different the spot must have been in past times from what it is now. And I always wonder that in all this aggregation of loveliness there should not be someone who combines literary talent with a fair face so that she might by her words further enhance the beauty of the hills and streams. Instead, all we see are these battalions of the powdered and mascaraed, robes scented, fans fluttering, circling in confused array with the hued clouds of twilight.

I once questioned the old people and discovered that some forty or fifty years ago Makuzugahara was not lined with teahouses and dance stages on both sides of the lane as it is now. During the Hōei era (1704–11), there was a woman named Okaji who opened a teahouse on the south side of the Gion cemetery. She loved to write Japanese poetry, and people who took an interest in such things collected her compositions in a work called the *Kaji-no-ha shū* or *Paper Mulberry Leaf Collection*. She had an adopted daughter named Yuri or Lily. Both women possessed great literary talent, and their names were known even among the court nobles. The Middle Counselor Reizei in particular treated them with deference and invited them to his home for an interview. The story of Yuri is especially worthy of being handed down.

I do not know where Yuri came from; some say she was from

Edo. She was highly intelligent and quick-witted; in matters of music or needlework she had only to be shown something once and she would understand it immediately. After she was adopted by Okaji, she began to copy her mother's literary pursuits and took great pleasure in composing poems. Each day she donned her madder robe and waited on customers, serving them their tea, but whenever she could steal a moment of leisure she would immediately take up brush and inkstone and write about the scent of the flowers, the chatter of the birds, taking for her theme whatever happened to confront her. She was not the kind who cared for a great deal of adornment and decoration, yet so attractive and fresh were the looks and form that Heaven had given her that, even in the lightest makeup and most ordinary clothes, she made a striking impression, and passersby never failed to halt their steps. Among the distinguished men of the capital and the sons of rich families there were many who pressed their attentions on her, while the boys who ordinarily had great confidence in their looks would add a daub of powder to their faces and scrutinize themselves in the mirror, hoping thereby to win Yuri's heart. But she took no notice of any of them.

The truth was that Yuri already had a young man named Tokuyama whom she had been intimate with for some time, the son of a samurai in the service of the Edo shogunate. He was a bright and talented fellow, but because of some affair he had had to leave Edo and had drifted to Kyoto, where he lived in great poverty, having no means to support himself. Yuri exhausted every resource at her command to help him, and as a result he was able to get by without want. Their affair went along in this manner for a year when she became pregnant and bore a daughter, which served greatly to increase the devotion the couple felt for each other.

It so happened that the heir to the head house of the Tokuyama family died, and the relatives, after debating on a suitable successor, sent a messenger with a letter to the young man inviting him to become heir. He wanted to take Yuri along with him when he returned to Edo, but she refused, saying, "You and I have been very close for ten years, and now in one morning to part like drifting duckweed or tumbling grasses will be a hard thing to bear indeed. But you are going home to a place of honor, and if you were to appear dragging some woman along with you, I'm afraid you would invite unfavorable comment."

The young man tried his best to persuade her, saying, "When I came to this city as a stranger and a homeless wanderer, it was due to your efforts alone that I escaped dying in some wayside ditch and have been able to survive until today. Now when I've suddenly become rich and eminent, I could not bear to cast aside the woman who shared the years of hardship with me!"

Yuri, however, was firm in her refusals. "I have enjoyed much love—more than I deserve—and it would be impossible for me not to leap with joy at the thought of accompanying you. The reason I cannot comply with your command is that you have been chosen to carry on the ancestral line of a distinguished family and must select a person of proper standing to be your mate. No mere roadside cherry or willow such as I would do for plucking. If I were to be so rash as to accompany you and prolong our alliance, I would bring disgrace not only to you, but to your ancestors as well—something that in my heart I am loath to do. Even if your kin out of pity were kind enough to let me remain as your concubine, should any trouble ensue, you would inevitably be drawn into the affair, and that too is a prospect that would cause me constant worry. I have pondered the matter deeply day and night, and I believe that parting from you today is the best way to insure a fitting close to the love and kindness you have shown me for these ten years. You must take

164

good care of yourself. I will say goodby now, goodby forever—please do not think of me any more!"

The young man did not venture to press her further, but expressed a desire to take his little daughter with him. Yuri replied, "You are still young and vigorous and when you find a new wife, you will surely in time be blessed with many children—no fear that in your old age you will lack the joy of young ones gathered about your knees. But I have vowed that once I part from you, I will never marry again—I will guard alone the blue-flamed lamp in my chamber. All I have to rely upon is this one child, and while I see her, I seem to see you as well. If she too is to leave me, I don't know how I can endure the days ahead!"

So in the end the man left the child with Yuri and went on his way. From this time on, Yuri was more circumspect than ever in her conduct, her only thought being the care and upbringing of her daughter. Mother and child lived a lonely life, yet each helped the other to keep going. When the girl grew up, she too proved to have artistic talent. Her name was Omachi. Yuri often would say to her, "Your father was a samurai. You must respect yourself as a woman—never look down on yourself!" Yuri's constant desire was to find a good husband for her daughter, but no one seemed to meet her requirements. There was, however, a young man named Ike who also lived at Makuzugahara and made a living selling his paintings and calligraphy, though he was very poor and scarcely managed to support himself. Others regarded him as of no consequence, but Yuri quite on her own made up her mind that he had great promise and in the end gave him her daughter in marriage.

Omachi soon learned her husband's business and acquired a considerable understanding of painting. Husband and wife would spend all day stretching paper and mixing inks, or would amuse themselves with koto playing and wine, and if at times they were so poor that dust collected in the rice steamer, they never showed the slightest concern. Yuri observed them with delight, saying, "My work is finished," and not long after took sick and died.

Some twenty or thirty years later, a samurai from the eastern region came inquiring for Mr. Ike. Leaving his attendants outside, he entered the gate alone. It happened that Ike was out and only his wife was at home. When she came to the door, the samurai asked, "Madam, are you the wife of Mr. Ike?" She replied that she was, whereupon he said, "In that case, you and I are half brother and sister—I am the son of Tokuyama So-and-so. I have wanted to meet you for a long time, but so many mountains and rivers block the way between here and Edo that I could make the journey in thought alone. Now, fortunately, official business has brought me here, and I can at last fulfill the wish I have cherished so long. I hope from now on we may visit back and forth from time to time and be on terms appropriate to brother and sister."

"As a matter of fact, I heard something of this from my mother before she died," said Ike's wife. "But she cautioned me that I was to have no social relations with the party in Edo. So, as much as I appreciate your generous intentions, I dare not go against the instructions she left." With this the samurai, looking very downcast, took his departure.

Mr. Ike in time became famous as a painter and calligrapher, and everyone throughout the country referred to him as Master Taiga. His wife Gyokuran was equally renowned as a painter, and people compared them to that devoted couple of ancient China, Liang Hung and his wife Meng Kuang. Gyokuran, of course, was none other than Yuri's daughter Omachi. A collection of Yuri's poems was put together after her death and has been handed down along with that of her mother Okaji. My friend Oku Dōitsu managed to get hold of a stray bit of Yuri's manuscript written in her own hand—the writing is very vigorous and forceful, like the woman herself.

In the course of various visits to Higashiyama I learned the details of Yuri's story from Geppō, a monk of Higashiyama, who recounted them for me. Originally I had been aware only that she was a woman of literary talent—how could I have known that she also possessed intelligence, virtue, and an exemplary ability to judge others? These days I see rich fellows and common fools, entranced with Taiga's reputation, all scrambling to buy up his paintings and calligraphy. But if they could somehow come face to face with Taiga himself, they would walk right by without ever recognizing him! Who among them would have the perception that Yuri did to single him out when he was living in dust and obscurity? Surely she deserves to be called an extraordinary woman. I'm afraid that people of later times will think she was in a class with the teahouse women of these days, who lounge against the door and vend their smiles. That is why I have written this biography of her.[1]

1. Ike no Taiga, regarded as one of the finest painters of the Tokugawa period, lived 1723 to 1776, his wife Gyokuran 1727 to 1784. The poems of Okaji, Yuri, and Gyokuran are preserved in a work known as the *Gion sanjo kashū* or "Collected Works of the Three Women Poets of Gion."

✍ The Biography of Oyuki

Oyuki or Snowflake was a lady swashbuckler of Osaka. It was in Osaka that General Hideyoshi built his fortress, and it remains a city of spirited and prodigal people who love to affect a rough and ready manner. Many citizens of Osaka have made names for themselves as cavaliers, but Snowflake was the only woman among them. She was the daughter of the mistress of a wealthy merchant of the Nagahori district, but from an early age was brought up by the Miyoshi family. The Miyoshi, who were also rich tradespeople, adopted a son whom they wished to marry to Snowflake, but she despised the boy as a puny weakling and would have none of it. At this time she took a vow never to marry. When her foster father died, she inherited the estate.

By nature Snowflake was of a high-spirited, gallant disposition. She devoted little attention to the family business, but studied calligraphy and painting with Yanagisawa Kien (1706–1758) and took lessons in swordmanship and judo. She was pale, large, and portly, with great strength in her limbs. Two women attendants named Tortoise (Okame) and Crag (Oiwa), both of whom were very strong and brave, constantly followed her about. At this time Snowflake had just turned sixteen, and her two companions were likewise in the bloom of their beauty. Young idlers and ruffians meeting them on the street would often tease the girls and challenge them to a battle. At such times Snowflake would glance meaningfully at her attendants, and they would thereupon knock the boys to the ground, often so hard that they could not get up again.

The place called Snake Slope in the southern suburbs was at this time very wild and deserted, and even in the daytime no one dared walk there. Snowflake once took a short cut through the spot when two robbers came upon her and tried to seize her sash, but she knocked them flat. In no time the story got around, and everyone stayed out of her way.

Snowflake, not having a husband, was ambitious to become a lady-in-waiting at court so that she could observe the life in the inner palace. Her excellent calligraphy won her a post as a clerk in the palace, which she occupied for five years; she was engaged in recording past events of the court. When she gave up this position, she shaved her head and became a nun, living in the Moon River Temple next door to the Shitennō-ji. . . . Snowflake customarily wore white clerical robes and continued as before to go wandering about with her two women companions.

Once when the temple was having an unveiling of the inner shrine and a great crowd of men and women had come to worship, it suddenly began to rain. Snowflake immediately bought over a thousand umbrellas and distributed them one to a person, though her supply soon ran out. On another occasion, when a memorial service was being held at the temple, she hired musicians to play and had the offerings prepared in very lavish fashion. When someone asked her the reason, she replied, "Today is the two hundredth anniversary of the death of my ancestor, Chancellor Hidetsugu!" She also presented a sum of money in private to the Hōkō-ji, a temple in Kyoto founded by General Hideyoshi, asking that it be used as a personal offering to the spirit of the general.[1] She was always giving herself such absurd airs.

1. Toyotomi Hideyoshi, the great military leader who unified Japan and built Osaka Castle, died in 1598. His adopted son Hidetsugu was forced to commit suicide in 1595, and his remaining heir was killed in the siege of Osaka Castle in 1615, when the Toyotomi family was wiped out. Oyuki's claim that she was related to these exalted personages was fanciful to say the least.

Her fortune eventually ran out and she built a little house in the village of Namba where she lived out the rest of her days. She bought a coffin and hung it up by the gate, and every day gathered with her friends to drink. One day she went out in the hot sun and dropped dead in the street. The villagers, recognizing her, carried her into the shop where she had always bought her wine, and rushed off to inform her household. Her corpse was prepared and laid away in the coffin. They buried her at the Temple of the Secret Spring in Namba. She was seventy-five when she died. Her gravestone was carved with the shape of a snowflake, as well as with that of a tortoise and a mountain crag, and is still in existence. From this it would appear that her two companions were buried with her. . . .

Master Kan Sazan came into possession of the manuscript of a poem in Chinese which the Confucian scholar Yanada Zeigan (1672–1757) had presented to Snowflake. Prizing it highly, he commissioned me to write a biography of her. Accordingly I have set forth the facts above. The story of Snowflake cannot, of course, be taken as a model of conduct. But in her time there were women who conducted themselves like men, while today we see only men who behave as women. My aim has been simply to divine in these events something of the rise and fall of Fortune, and to ellicit, perhaps, a sigh.

Part 4

WORKS BY NATSUME SŌSEKI

Natsume Sōseki (1867–1916), one of the greatest novelists of modern Japan, in his youth in Tokyo devoted several years to intensive study of Chinese language and literature, in which he took a deep interest. As a student in the Preliminary School to Tokyo Imperial University (later renamed the First Higher Middle School), he was a classmate of Masaoka Shiki (see p. 82), and the two composed poetry and prose in Chinese and showed their works to each other for criticism. Though Sōseki in the meantime had taken up the study of English, and for a while became a lecturer in English literature at Tokyo Imperial University, he continued throughout his life to write *kanshi*, and was particularly active in the medium in 1916, shortly before his death on December 9th from a stomach ulcer. He was a great admirer of the works of the Zen priest-poet Ryōkan, and many of his poems reflect his interest in Zen and are philosophical in nature. Most of his *kanshi* bear the heading *mudai* or "untitled." My selection from Sōseki's Chinese writings begins with excerpts from the *Bokusetsuroku* or "Record of Chips and Shavings," a *kambun* account of a trip to the Bōsō Peninsula in Chiba Prefecture which Sōseki wrote in the autumn of 1889. Chiba comprises the old provinces of Awa, Shimōsa, and Kazusa. My translation represents about half of the original, which is interspersed with poems in *shih* form and one brief *fu* or rhyme-prose.

Excerpts from the "Record of Chips and Shavings" (Bokusetsuroku)

When I was a boy I memorized thousands of T'ang and Sung works and loved to compose in Chinese. Sometimes I strained my ingenuity, polishing and refining and spending ten days to get one piece into shape; at other times the words just came tumbling out of my mouth, and I was sure I had achieved a fine flavor of naturalness and simplicity. I began to ask myself if there was any reason why I shouldn't be able to write as well as the men of past times, and eventually I made up my mind to pursue a literary career. From then on, whenever I went on an outing or climbed up to some high place to view the scenery, I always composed a record of the occasion. Two or three years later, I opened the box, took out the numerous pieces I had written, and read them over. Those I had formerly thought of as highly ingenious and impeccably polished turned out to be total failures, fussy and overrefined, and those I had previously regarded as simple and direct now appeared hopelessly contrived and obscure. In terms of persons, they were at times like a wistful geisha, breathless and wilting, at times like a headstrong boy brashly trying to outdo his elders. Not a one was worth looking at. I tore the paper to bits, burned the manuscripts, blushing with shame, and for a long time felt completely downcast.

Then I said to myself with a sigh, the men of ancient times read tens of thousands of books and took journeys tens of thousands of miles long—that's why their writings have such power and breadth, why they are so unmistakably superior in vigor and tone! Now here I am, timorous and hesitant-stepped, always sticking close to the home of my father and mother and never setting foot outside the city—and yet I expect my writings to reach the heights attained by the ancients. How absurd! Thereupon I resolutely determined to don traveler's sandals and set off on distant wanderings. But before I could carry out my ambitions, there was a complete change in my circumstances. I found myself tucking books with sidewise crab-walk Western writing in them under my arm and setting off for school, and my school lessons kept me so incessantly busy that I had no more leisure to read the bird-track writings of the East.[1] All my books of Chinese lyrics and rhyme-prose, letters and essays had to be heartlessly bundled up and put away on the top shelf. I had no more chance even to write the kind of overrefined and obscure pieces I had formerly produced, much less try to emulate the writers of the past.

In the twentieth year of Meiji (1887) I finally put on a big straw hat and climbed Mount Fuji. Crossing Hakone, I pushed through swirls of white cloud, boots trampling over several feet of piled snow, the soles of my feet frozen, my fingers chapped. I gazed far off at the mountains of the eight provinces around me and found them like little lumps of earth. My spirits soared grandly upward as though to overtop the clouds, and yet I was unable to compose even one piece to commemorate such a splendid journey. Again in July of this year (1889) my elder brother and I took a trip to Okitsu in Shizuoka. The region is one of the most famous spots on the eastern sea, and we stayed there over ten days, completely at leisure and with nothing to do, but in the end I couldn't write a single poem or passage of prose. Piti-

1. In September of 1883 Sōseki entered the Seiritsu Gakusha in Tokyo in order to prepare for the entrance examination of the Preliminary School to Tokyo Imperial University. At this time he began the study of English.

ful! In the past I wanted to write but I didn't have any famous mountains and great rivers to stir me to inspiration. But now I've viewed the famous mountains and great rivers and I don't have one word to show for all that fine scenery—it must be fate!

In August I set out again, crossing the straits by boat for a trip to the province of Awa. I climbed Saw Mountain, tramped through the provinces of Shimōsa and Kazusa, went up the Tone River and thus made my way back to Tokyo. The trip took thirty days and covered over ninety *ri*. As soon as I got home the autumn rains began, and for days on end I sat in my room idle, thinking over the delights and hardships of the journey, until I couldn't contain myself any longer. Then I picked up a brush and began writing, continuing until I had piled up a number of sheets. I hope this may in a small way help to compensate for those earlier times when I wrote pieces without taking any journeys, or took journeys without producing any writings. But by now I have abandoned my literary ambitions, and because this was written entirely in spare moments, it is of course as fussy and obscure as my other pieces. To call attention to its trite and commonplace nature, I have titled it "Chips and Shavings." [2]

I started out on August 7th. The day was extremely windy and nearly all the people in the boat were seasick and apprehensive, but there were three girls sitting on the deck talking and laughing as though nothing were amiss. I felt deeply ashamed that a grown man like myself should be no match for these kerchiefed females, and I forced myself to go sit down in a formal position with my back against the rail, intending to observe

2. Years later, Sōseki used the piece as the basis for his description of a similar journey taken by Sensei and "K" in the last section of his famous novel *Kokoro*. Sōseki made the trip with classmates from the First Higher Middle School.

the battle that was going on between the wind and the waves. Just as I was staggering to my feet again, a violent wave lifted up the boat, sloshing it sideways until it almost capsized. I lost my footing and stumbled forward, and at that moment a fierce blast of wind came along, snatched off my cap, and blew it away. Turning to look, I could see my lost cap whirling and tumbling into the distance amidst the flying spray. All the boatmen clapped their hands and laughed uproariously, and the three girls joined in with what sounded like a loud guffaw. I was utterly chagrined at having cut such a sorry figure.

From the time I reached Awa, I went bathing in the salt water at least two or three times a day, and sometimes as many as five or six times. When I went in swimming I made a point of leaping and splashing around like a little boy at play, hoping that way to work up a good appetite. When I felt tired, I stretched out on my side on the hot sand. As the warmth soaked into my stomach, I had a wonderful feeling of contentment. After a few days of this, my hair began to turn russet and my skin to turn yellow. After ten days, the russet had turned to red and the yellow to black. Standing before the mirror, I was completely dumbfounded at the way I looked. . . .

The group making the trip with me consisted of five boys including myself. None of the others knew anything about writing prose or poetry. Sometimes they drank sake and made a loud noise, at other times they bantered away endlessly, alarming the maid who brought us our meals. As soon as we came in from swimming, they would gather around for a game of chess or play cards to pass the time. I alone sat lost in deep meditation, my thoughts roaming far away, and sometimes I mumbled and groaned as though I were in great pain. The others all thought my failure to laugh was some peculiar affectation, but I paid no attention to them. The Ch'ing writer Li Lung-o (mid-

19th cen.), when he was mulling over his thoughts, used to appear to be in great pain, but once a piece was finished he was so overjoyed he would yank at his clothes and run around the couch hooting wildly. When I mumble and groan, I'm going through the same sort of process, though bystanders don't realize this. . . .

What I've seen of Awa has been about two-thirds mountains, not particularly high but thrusting up steep and sharp into the sky, rocky and with no layer of soil for the trees to cling to. . . . To the northeast [3] is a range that angles back and forth, cutting right across the peninsula—this has the highest and steepest peaks. Viewing the rows of pinnacles from a distance, they look like the teeth of a saw pointing up at the blue sky, and in fact are called Nokogiriyama or Saw Mountain. . . . The lowest peak on the western end is named Moon Ring Peak. The temple known as the Nihon-ji is situated halfway up the peak. In the reign of Emperor Shōmu the monk Gyōgi (668–749), complying with an imperial command, journeyed to eastern Japan and, viewing this mountain, declared it a realm of true spirituality. He proceeded to open a trail to the mountain and found a temple of twelve cloisters and one hundred subtemples. In the years following, such famous monks as Rōben (689–773), Kūkai (774–835), and Ennin (794–864) visited it, and the images they carved are still there today. Later it fell to ruin and was rebuilt a number of times. During the An'ei era (1772–80) the priest Guden imported stone from Izu and commissioned a stonecutter to fashion images of *rakan* or arhats. Added to the earlier statues carved by Kūkai and others, they made a total of 1,503 images set in place on the mountain. From that time on, the temple became famous for its *rakan* statues. . . .

3. I.e., northeast of Hota on the western shore of the peninsula, the port where Sōseki landed.

In August of 1889, my friends and I climbed up, following a trail along a stream for some five hundred paces until we reached the temple gate. The plaster had crumbled and fallen, the tiles were scattered, the railings broken, and visitors had written their names all over the walls, the leaves of the gates being so covered with scrawls it was impossible to read what was written on them. After climbing twenty or thirty paces more, we came to a small pond with shady willows surrounding it and pink lotuses on its quiet water. When the mountain breeze passed over the lotus leaves, they stirred slightly, the beads of dew on them rolling and swaying gently, seeming about to roll off but never quite doing so. We circled the pond and then, turning left, climbed several flights of stone steps till we came to a flat area twenty or thirty yards square shaded with dense clumps of plantain and parasol trees. There were two small huts in the midst with thatched roofs and bamboo lattice windows, like farmers' huts. When we asked our guide, he said that they were where the temple monks lived. The sun by this time was high in the sky, but the gates and doors were shut tight and the place looked completely deserted. The guide said that at the time of the Restoration the government had confiscated all the temple's houses and lands and that it had by now all but gone out of existence. I wandered through the dense shade cast by the twining branches, imagining how, long ago, the black-robed monks and the priests in their splendid brocade vestments must have passed along the vermilion passageways and up and down the painted stairs, for a long time lost in melancholy thought.

The grass in front of the huts was as soft as a carpet, and through gaps in the jagged slope we could see glimpses of the ocean far away, with soaring birds and wind-filled sails standing out sharp against it. We followed the trail up the slope as it grew steadily steeper, till we were clinging to the rocks and vines to make our way upward. Far above we could see the stone statues ranged in intricate files on top of the cliff. We tried to hurry forward, but we kept losing the trail as it wound this way and that with each turn of the cliff, and it was only after a number of false starts and the space of an hour or so that we finally succeeded in reaching the statues. The tallest were three feet, the smallest one foot. The faces of some had been eroded away beyond recognition, others had been mutilated by visitors and were missing a head or a limb, but more than a hundred were still in complete condition. Each had a distinctive face and form, no two alike—you could see how thoughtfully the carver had done his work. He had also placed them in such a way that they were not all clumped together side by side. The visitor first saw some two hundred stone images and assumed that these were the finest of the *rakan*. But then, as he rounded the corner of the cliff, he suddenly came on another hundred or more images. Looking up, he saw a gigantic cluster of peaks almost collapsing on him, and as he was about to step aside in fear, his eyes would light on another twenty or thirty images perched on top of the peaks. At another point, at the head of a ravine where the path ended, there was a cave, and the whole cave was filled with *rakan* statues! The mountain trail is so steep and irregular that there was no level ground on which to line up the images. As it is, the visitor keeps changing his angle of view with each step, and is all the more delighted with the manner in which the splendid sights are offered to his eye.

By noon we reached the crest of the mountain and rested. The surrounding hills that earlier had seemed half hidden in clouds now all lay at our feet and we could see just how the range twisted and turned, rose and fell. Since coming to Awa I've looked off into the distance at Saw Mountain morning and evening but I never knew it was this high and steep. . . .

Tanjō-ji is in Kominato in Awa. Nichiren (1222–82), the founder of the Lotus Sutra sect of Buddhism, was born there, and men of later times established a temple at the site where his hut had stood—hence it is called Tanjō-ji or the Temple of the Birth. With mountains behind it, it faces the sea, where the tides come tumbling and surging in, flooding to the full and then ebbing out again. This is the spot called Tai-no-ura or Sea Bream Bay. We had already heard much about its wonders when we were in Tokyo, so we hired a boat and pushed off. When we had gone several hundred yards from shore we came to a shoal of sharp rocks blocking the passage of the boat. As the great sea swells came angling and rolling in, they would strike the rocks with a fierce fury, as though to seize them and fling them away, and when they found this impossible, they would leap up and tumble over them. Jets of white spray shot upward, casting their reflection over the blue waves and shining with a confusion of colors. There were birds perched on the rocks with red crowns and black legs—some species I didn't know the name of. When a billow would strike they would fly up and circle low above the water, waiting for the wave to subside, and then would alight on the rocks again. My friends and I kept shouting and exclaiming at the sight, whereupon the boatman laughed and said, "This is nothing—I'll show you something that will really surprise you!" Then he ordered his companion to take a dipper and stand in the prow, while he remained in the stern working the scull. The dipper was five inches square and filled with hundreds of sardines. The dipper had a handle five feet long, and the man standing in the prow held the end of it as though preparing to shake the dipper and dump the sardines into the water. While he waited for further orders, the boatman turned to us and said, "Just keep your eyes on the water!" I accordingly leaned on the side of the boat and stared intently down at the sea. Then the boatman shouted, "Scatter the sardines!" He had no sooner given the order than brocade-like patterns suddenly appeared deep down in the water and began to move and cluster together. As they came gradually closer, we could see that they were hundreds of fins pushing through the waves and swooping upward, fighting to get at the sardines. It was noon and the burning rays of the sun beat down on the waves. Flashes of fire shone from the waves, and in their midst the bright red of the patterned fish scales would appear and disappear. Some of the fish rolled to the surface, baring the whiskers on their chins, others leaped up until their heads were clear of the water. A dazzling radiance surrounded the boat for a space of several paces; in a single moment everything turned the color of gold. "Ordinarily the fishing boats have to go out three or four miles before they can get bream," the boatman told us. "To find such schools of them right here only a few hundred yards from shore is a real marvel! And another marvel is the way they fight for sardines without any fear of people! But a few waves slapping at the rocks and the wind and water tussling together—that you can see anywhere. No reason to make a fuss over that!"

After we left the boat we went to the Tanjō-ji to look at the paintings and documents in its possession, twenty or thirty items. Most of them are things written by Nichiren. The monk said, "When the Master was born, his family caught two bream at the shore. The following day the same thing happened, and so on for a total of seven days. Since that time the local people out of respect for the Master have never dared to catch bream. . . . And if anyone on the sly catches a bream and eats it, he is sure to sicken and die of the fever!" . . .

✍ Self-derision: Appended to "Chips and Shavings"

With hateful eyes I wait withdrawal from the world,
lazy, with this doltish ignorance, to try its fame.
Turning my back upon the days, I slander contemporaries;
I read old books to curse the ancients.
With the talent of a donkey, a lagging roan,
head vacuous as the autumn locust's shell,
abounding only in passion for the mists,
I shall rate rivers, from my rude hut classify the hills.[4]

4. It is significant that Sōseki at the age of twenty-two was already talking of withdrawing from the world and living the hermit life so often extolled in Chinese Six Dynasties poetry. The literary name Sōseki, which he adopted around 1903, derives from an anecdote concerning one such Chinese recluse, Sun Ch'u of the third century A.D. Though Sōseki never became a recluse, his critical attitude toward the society of his time is apparent in his rejection of the honorary doctorate offered him by the Ministry of Education in 1911, and in numerous other acts, as well as in such works as *Botchan*.

✍ Untitled

(Written in the hospital after a severe stomach illness; 1910.)

I spat up streams of crimson blood, my bowels' own writing,
rich patterns surging, lighting up the dusk.
By evening it seemed my whole body had turned to bone;
on the bed I lay rock-like, dreaming of icy clouds.

⚖ Untitled

(August 16, 1916)

I have no mind to bow to the Buddha, peer into the heart;
faced with monks in a mountain temple, my thoughts race to
    poetry.
A hundred years, pine and cypress encircle the walls before
    fading;
creeper and vine in one day come clambering over the fence.
Words of doctrine—but who lights the lamp before the grotto?
Dharma hymns—what power have they to burnish the moss on
    the stone?
Let me ask the patched-robed monk practising his Zen:
these hill-blue mists—what surface have they for defiling
    dust to cling to?

✍ Untitled

(October 6, 1916)

Not a Christian, not a Buddhist, not a Confucian either,
in a blind lane peddling my writings, I managed to amuse my-
    self.
What fragrance did I gather, passing through the gardens of art?
How many greens have I wandered, there on poetry fields?
In the ashes of the burned book the book lives, I know;
in Dharma-less worlds the Dharma may spring to life again.
Beat the gods till they're dead, and when no shadow remains,
clear, sharp in the formless void, wise and foolish will appear.

✍ Untitled

(A set of three poems; October 21, 1916)

Once I was the master of a city;
I burned the city down, walked through its broad streets,
on and on, shedding excess things—
Where to throw away my ignorance?

Once I was a homeless dog,
straying over the grass-grown moor;
the little boys—they didn't mean to—beat me to death—
When will I enter the gates of home?

Once I was a boy in brocaded robes;
I sold the robes, sold my pearls too,
but this lanky body no trader will buy—
stark naked, a naked fool!

✍ Untitled

(A set of three poems; October 22, 1916)

Once I was a poor man's son,
envying the gates of the rich and lordly;
one morning they filled my empty belly—
I died on the spot to requite their kindness.

Once I lived in the house to the east;
I went to beg food from my western neighbor;
went, came home, and what did I see?
My old hut in the pouring rain.

Once I was the child of a peaceful age,
contented, forgetful of parting and strife;
suddenly the fires of war blazed up—
I died, and found my hunger for the first time healed.

✍ Untitled

(November 20, 1916)

The true path is shadowy and still, far away and hard to find;
embracing none but empty thoughts, let me walk through past
    and present.
Emerald waters, emerald hills—what do they know of ego?
Sheltering heaven, sheltering earth, there is only mindlessness.
Uncertain colors of evening: a moon parting from the grass;
restless voice of autumn: wind that inhabits the forest.
Eyes, ears both forgotten, my body too is lost;
alone in the void I sing a song of white clouds.

Index of Authors

Chūgan Engetsu, 28-30
Ema Saikō, 58
Fujii Chikugai, 60-62
Fujita Koshirō, 70
Gensei, Priest, 31-32
Gesshō, Priest, 67
Itō Jinsai, 33
Itō Tōgai, 34
Kaga no Chiyo, 39
Kametani Seiken, 80
Kan Sazan, 42-47
Kikuchi Gozan, 51
Kokan Shiren, 25-27
Masaoka Shiki, 82
Mokurai, Priest, 79
Murakami Bussan, 64
Nakajima Sōin, 52
Narushima Ryūhoku, 75-78
Natsume Sōseki, 173-89
Nogi Maresuke, 81
Ogasawara Gokyō, 73

Ōkubo Shibutsu, 50
Ōzaki Bunki, 59
Rai Kyōhei, 48
Rai Mikisaburō, 68-69
Rai San'yō, 121-70
Rokunyo (Rikunyo), Priest, 37-41
Ryōkan, 87-117
Sahara Morizumi, 71
Sakuma Shōzan, 66
Sūkatan, 11
Takeuchi Untō, 63
Tani Rokkoku, 35
Tate Ryūwan, 49
Terakado Seiken, 53-54
Tomobayashi Mitsuhira, 65
Tsuchiya Kyūtai, 84
Yabu Kozan, 36
Yaguchi Kensai, 74
Yanagawa Kōran, 57
Yanagawa Seigan, 55-56

Translations from the Oriental Classics

Major Plays of Chikamatsu, tr. Donald Keene   1961
Records of the Grand Historian of China, translated from the
    Shih chi of Ssu-ma Ch'ien, tr. Burton Watson, 2 vols.   1961
Instructions for Practical Living and Other Neo-Confucian
    Writings by Wang Yang-ming, tr. Wing-tsit Chan   1963
Chuang Tzu: Basic Writings, tr. Burton Watson, paper-
    back ed. only   1964
The Mahābhārata, tr. Chakravarthi V. Narasimhan   1965
The Manyōshū, Nippon Gakujutsu Shinkōkai edition   1965
Su Tung-p'o: Selections from a Sung Dynasty Poet, tr. Burton
    Watson   1965
Bhartrihari: Poems, tr. Barbara Stoler Miller. Also in pa-
    perback ed.   1967
Basic Writings of Mo Tzu, Hsün Tzu, and Han Fei Tzu, tr.
    Burton Watson. Also in separate paperback eds.   1967
The Awakening of Faith, attributed to Aśvaghosha, tr. Yo-
    shito S. Hakeda   1967
Reflections on Things at Hand: The Neo-Confucian Anthology,
    comp. Chu Hsi and Lü Tsu-ch'ien, tr. Wing-tsit Chan   1967
The Platform Sutra of the Sixth Patriarch, tr. Philip B.
    Yampolsky   1967
Essays in Idleness: The Tsurezuregusa of Kenkō, tr. Donald
    Keene   1967
The Pillow Book of Sei Shōnagon, tr. Ivan Morris, 2 vols.   1967
Two Plays of Ancient India: The Little Clay Cart and the
    Minister's Seal, tr. J. A. B. van Buitenen   1968
The Complete Works of Chuang Tzu, tr. Burton Watson   1968
The Romance of the Western Chamber (Hsi Hsiang chi) tr. S.
    I. Hsiung   1968

The Manyōshū, Nippon Gakujutsu Shinkōkai edition. Paperback text edition. 1969

Records of the Historian: Chapters from the Shih chi of Ssu-ma Ch'ien. Paperback text edition, tr. Burton Watson 1969

Cold Mountain: 100 Poems by the T'ang Poet Han-shan, tr. Burton Watson. Also in paperback ed. 1970

Twenty Plays of the Nō Theatre, ed. Donald Keene. Also in paperback ed. 1970

Chūshingura: The Treasury of Loyal Retainers, tr. Donald Keene 1971

The Zen Master Hakuin: Selected Writings, tr. Philip B. Yampolsky 1971

Chinese Rhyme-Prose, tr. Burton Watson 1971

Kūkai: Major Works, tr. Yoshito S. Hakeda 1972

The Old Man Who Does as He Pleases: Selections from the Poetry and Prose of Lu Yu, tr. Burton Watson 1973

The Lion's Roar of Queen Śrīmālā, tr. Alex & Hideko Wayman 1974

Courtier and Commoner in Ancient China: Selections from the History of The Former Han by Pan Ku, tr. Burton Watson 1974

Japanese Literature in Chinese. Vol. I: Poetry and Prose in Chinese by Japanese Writers of the Early Period, tr. Burton Watson 1975

Japanese Literature in Chinese. Vol. II: Poetry and Prose in Chinese by Japanese Writers of the Later Period, tr. Burton Watson 1976

Scripture of the Lotus Blossom of the Fine Dharma, tr. Leon Hurvitz 1976

Studies In Oriental Culture

1. *The Ōnin War: History of Its Origins and Background, with a Selective Translation of the Chronicle of Ōnin*, by H. Paul Varley   1967
2. *Chinese Government in Ming Times: Seven Studies*, ed. Charles O. Hucker   1969
3. *The Actors' Analects (Yakusha Rongo)*, ed. and tr. by Charles J. Dunn and Bunzō Torigoe   1969
4. *Self and Society in Ming Thought*, by Wm. Theodore de Bary and the Conference on Ming Thought   1970
5. *A History of Islamic Philosophy*, by Majid Fakhry   1970
6. *Phantasies of a Love Thief: The Caurapañcāśikā Attributed to Bilhana*, by Barbara S. Miller   1971
7. *Iqbal: Poet-Philosopher of Pakistan*, ed. Hafeez Malik   1971
8. *The Golden Tradition: An Anthology of Urdu Poetry*, by Ahmed Ali   1973
9. *Conquerors and Confucians: Aspects of Political Change in Late Yüan China*, by John W. Dardess   1973
10. *The Unfolding of Neo-Confucianism*, by Wm. Theodore de Bary and the Conference on Seventeenth-Century Chinese Thought   1975
11. *To Acquire Wisdom: The Way of Wang Yang-ming*, by Julia Ching   1976
12. *Gods, Priests, and Warriors: The Bhrgus of the Mahābhārata*, by Robert P. Goldman   1976
13. *Mei Yao-ch'en and the Development of Early Sung Poetry*, by Jonathan Chaves   1976

Companions To Asian Studies

Approaches to the Oriental Classics, ed. Wm. Theodore de
Bary   1959
Early Chinese Literature, by Burton Watson   1962
Approaches to Asian Civilizations, ed. Wm. Theodore de
Bary and Ainslie T. Embree   1964
The Classic Chinese Novel: A Critical Introduction, by C. T.
Hsia   1968
*Chinese Lyricism: Shih Poetry from the Second to the Twelfth
Century,* tr. Burton Watson   1971
A Syllabus of Indian Civilization, by Leonard A. Gordon
and Barbara Stoler Miller   1971
Twentieth-Century Chinese Stories, ed. C. T. Hsia and Jo-
seph S. M. Lau   1971
A Syllabus of Chinese Civilization, by J. Mason Gentzler,
2d ed.   1972
A Syllabus of Japanese Civilization, by H. Paul Varley, 2d
ed.   1972
An Introduction to Chinese Civilization, ed. John Meskill,
with the assistance of J. Mason Gentzler   1973
An Introduction to Japanese Civilization, ed. Arthur E. Tie-
demann   1974
A Guide to Oriental Classics, ed. Wm. Theodore de Bary
and Ainslie T. Embree, 2d ed.   1975

Introduction To Oriental Civilizations

Wm. Theodore de Bary, *Editor*

Sources of Japanese Tradition   1958   Paperback ed., 2 vols.   1964
Sources of Indian Tradition   1958   Paperback ed., 2 vols.   1964
Sources of Chinese Tradition   1960   Paperback ed., 2 vols.   1964